Praise for *Huma*

C000135151

'The latest pithy, socio-techno commentary from authors Daniel Newman and Olivier Blanchard incisively cleaves the controversy and daunting surroundings of how AI and greater machine automation will affect people, businesses, and societies. Through the study of how leading technology companies are working to bring about (and employ) AI, they suggest that the "A" in AI is indeed not an "S" for synthetic or substitution, but rather an "A" for assistance and augmentation. I enthusiastically encourage you to read this clever and sometimes humorous exploration to help you refine your vision of the coming AI revolution.' HERNS PIERRE-JEROME, DIRECTOR, GLOBAL INDUSTRY ANALYST RELATIONSHIPS, QUALCOMM INCORPORATED

'Newman and Blanchard offer an insightful and balanced assessment of the opportunities and risks as AI becomes pervasive in our everyday lives. Despite the divided world vision on both the potential and risks, we all have common ground on the need to transform, which came through in Dell Technologies' Realizing 2030 study. The future is bright for AI to augment, not replace, human potential, leading to a fruitful human–machine partnership.' JASON SHEPHERD, IOT AND EDGE COMPUTING CTO, DELL TECHNOLOGIES

'Daniel Newman and Olivier Blanchard have a unique combination of experience, insight and strategic vision. *Human/Machine* combines practical experiences from senior executives of innovative organizations with deep industry insight gleaned from thoughtful research with the ability to spot new mega trends. Their work in the burgeoning field of smart automation and AI puts them in the highest echelons of opinion leaders shaping the narrative around this nascent technology field.' STEVEN DICKENS, GLOBAL OFFERING MANAGER, IBM SYSTEMS

'At UiPath, we are enabling a future where employees are empowered to automate tedious and time-consuming work, allowing them to focus on creative and challenging problems, and we are driven by the enormous potential for our platform to be the gateway to transform our customers' digital business operations with AI and machine learning. I'm confident that you will find *Human/Machine* both informative and thought provoking and hope it inspires readers to take the time to better capture and learn from the information that runs through their organizations, customers and partners.' BOBBY PATRICK, CMO, UIPATH

'AI, automation and the impact they will have on the future of work has become one of the high-tech industry's hottest topics. *Human/Machine* provided me with a valuable, balanced perspective on the impact that human–machine partnerships will have on both work and our society.' PATRICK MOORHEAD, PRESIDENT, MOOR INSIGHTS & STRATEGY AND TOP-RANKED GLOBAL TECH INDUSTRY ANALYST

Human/Machine

*The future of our partnership
with machines*

Daniel Newman
Olivier Blanchard

Kogan Page
INSPIRE

Publisher's note

Every possible effort has been made to ensure that the information contained in this book is accurate at the time of going to press, and the publishers and authors cannot accept responsibility for any errors or omissions, however caused. No responsibility for loss or damage occasioned to any person acting, or refraining from action, as a result of the material in this publication can be accepted by the editor, the publisher or the authors.

First published in Great Britain and the United States in 2019 by Kogan Page Limited

Apart from any fair dealing for the purposes of research or private study, or criticism or review, as permitted under the Copyright, Designs and Patents Act 1988, this publication may only be reproduced, stored or transmitted, in any form or by any means, with the prior permission in writing of the publishers, or in the case of reprographic reproduction in accordance with the terms and licences issued by the CLA. Enquiries concerning reproduction outside these terms should be sent to the publishers at the undermentioned addresses:

2nd Floor, 45 Gee Street	122 W 27th St, 10th Floor	4737/23 Ansari Road
London	New York, NY 10001	Daryaganj
EC1V 3RS	USA	New Delhi 110002
United Kingdom		India

www.koganpage.com

© Daniel Newman and Olivier Blanchard, 2019

The right of Daniel Newman and Olivier Blanchard to be identified as the authors of this work has been asserted by them in accordance with the Copyright, Designs and Patents Act 1988.

ISBNs

Hardback	978 0 7494 9810 8
Paperback	978 0 7494 8424 8
Ebook	978 0 7494 8425 5

British Library Cataloguing-in-Publication Data

A CIP record for this book is available from the British Library.

Library of Congress Cataloging-in-Publication Number

2019020803

Typeset by Integra Software Services, Pondicherry
Print production managed by Jellyfish
Printed and bound by CPI Group (UK) Ltd, Croydon, CR0 4YY

Contents

About the authors xi
Acknowledgements xiii

1 **A short history of human–machine partnerships** 1

From tools to enhancements to early partnerships: a recap of
the last few million years 1

Smart automation: a new pivot 5

Understanding the impact of automation on employment 7

Reminder: real-world AI is not movie AI 9

An example: how might smart automation in transportation
affect professional drivers? 10

Task automation vs *job* automation: a key to understanding the
future of human–machine partnerships 12

New tools, enhancements and human–machine partnerships:
what to expect next 14

Smart automation and job consolidation: who is most at
risk? 16

Automation as a means of *increasing* human potential: which
traits and skills will automation help promote in human
workers? 21

Shifting human capital from low-value tasks to high-value
tasks 23

Human–machine partnerships as an intuitive and balanced
evolutionary response to smart automation 25

2 **The state of human–machine partnerships** 29

Evaluating human–machine partnerships: the importance of
finding common ground 29

Evaluating human–machine partnerships: from cost–benefit
thinking to cause-and-effect modelling 31

How human–machine partnerships create disruption   38
What will the future look like?   40
How machines can help us become better at adapting to
   change   42
The value of human–machine partnerships in a nutshell   44

3 **Framing expectations for the next age of human–machine
   partnerships**   47

What's next for human–machine partnerships?   47
Beyond the next 10 years   52
What does this mean for businesses?   54
What does this mean for workers?   57
What does this mean for the world's education and training
   infrastructure?   60
What does this mean for consumers?   61
What does this mean for technology companies?   62

4 **How businesses should prepare for the next age of human–
   machine partnerships**   65

The 10-year digital transformation roadmap   65
Three steps to transforming your business   69
Applying change management principles to the
   coming shift   71
Finding the right balance between automation and
   augmentation   73
IT and HR: a new chapter in internal collaboration   76
What types of human–machine partnerships should businesses
   prioritize?   79
Hiring and training for a new class of machine-adjacent
   roles   92
How SMBs/SMEs will benefit from more synergy between
   humans and machines   94

5 How workers should prepare for the next age of human–machine partnerships 97

Futureproofing careers in the age of smart automation 97
Awareness, initiative and resources: an adaptation
  playbook 100
Embracing technology partnerships and augmentation: none of
  this is about humans vs machines 102
Augmenting yourself towards becoming a more valuable
  worker 103
From white-collar and blue-collar jobs to next-collar jobs, and
  back again: what colour will the collars of tomorrow
  be? 104
Competing in a world of augmented workers and technologists:
  how professionals should leverage smart automation to
  increase their value 105
Building your own next-collar job toolkit 108
Specific advice for key job categories 113
In closing 124

6 How educational institutions should prepare for the next age
of human–machine partnerships 127

Leaving 20th-century education behind 127
Separating education and job training: practical
  considerations 128

7 How consumers should prepare for the next age of human–machine partnerships 153

How human-machine partnerships will impact our
  daily lives 153
From search engines to recommendation engines 154
Why trust is the next killer app 156
Where consumer-facing human–machine partnerships go from
  here: welcome to the age of 'AI inside' 157

How will smart automation and AI help drive smart home automation? 160

How will smart automation and AI impact transportation and infrastructure? 163

How will smart automation and AI transform the way we shop? 167

How will smart automation and AI shape the future of healthcare and homecare? 171

What will be the impact of smart automation and AI on our lifestyles and relationships? 176

How will smart automation and AI impact the way consumers think about life planning? 179

How should we protect our personal safety and privacy in the age of smart automation and AI? 180

A final observation 183

8 How technology companies should prepare for the next age of human–machine partnerships 185

Asking the right questions: do technology companies have a duty to minimize harm in the pursuit of progress? 185

Technology and responsibility: the duty of not creating monsters 186

Why technology fluency must live at the core of all technology oversight 188

How to ensure that your Big Butler and/or Big Mother company does not become a Big Brother company 189

How to apply these philosophical questions to the problem of job loss related to automation 190

Important questions to ask 193

Designing for the three primary categories of automation solutions: Big Brother, Big Mother and Big Butler 196

Fear and loathing in machine learning: why designing for augmentation rather than automation might make more sense, at least for now 200

9 The future of human–machine partnerships: Putting it all together   207

Reframing the discussion: automation is not the enemy… as long as we don't make it our enemy   207

A vision of the future of automation that we can all benefit from   209

What it may take to make automation work at scale for society   221

Big Brother, Big Mother, and Big Butler: why designing the future matters, and why we cannot afford to leave intent to chance   228

Driving towards a Big Mother- and Big Butler-inspired future of human–machine partnerships   231

Notes   235
Index   239

About the authors

Daniel Newman is the Principal Analyst of Futurum Research and the CEO of Broadsuite Media Group. He works with the world's largest technology brands exploring digital transformation and how it is influencing the enterprise and is regularly cited in *The Times*, Barron's, TechCrunch and CNBC and is a *Forbes* and *MarketWatch* contributor.

Olivier Blanchard is a Senior Analyst with Futurum Research, where he focuses on the impact of emerging and disruptive technologies including artificial intelligence, the Internet of Things, smart automation, edge compute and robotics. He is the author of *Social Media ROI* and, with Daniel Newman, co-author of *Building Dragons,* and *Futureproof.*

Acknowledgements

The ideas, case examples, approaches and forward-looking concepts shared in this book came from years of dialogue with practitioners, successes from our practices, and professional work from organizations we partner with and learn from every day. Those who have contributed directly or indirectly to this endeavour have our fullest gratitude.

We particularly wish to thank the amazing companies that we work with, that we drew examples from, and especially those that provided us with insights for this book. In no particular order: Apple, Dell, Cisco, IBM, Qualcomm, Intel, Microsoft, HP, HPE, Samsung, SAP, SAS, Dassault Systèmes, Facebook, Google, Amazon, Automation Anywhere and UiPath.

We also wish to thank our families for sharing our crazy journey, supporting our endeavours, and being more than patient with us when our work takes us away from them. We could not do this without them.

CHAPTER ONE

A short history of human–machine partnerships

From tools to enhancements to early partnerships: a recap of the last few million years

'Will a machine take away my job?' That is the question that first inspired us to write this book. Is a future increasingly driven by smart automation and artificial intelligence incompatible with a future in which human beings are able to work in the sorts of jobs that fulfil them, allow them to pursue their interests and ambitions, and also enable them to achieve, at the very minimum, some degree of financial security – if not financial independence? Will machines replace human workers? Perhaps more to the point, will machines make humans *obsolete*?

There is no simple answer to those questions, but there is good evidence to suggest that, despite countless alarmist articles to the contrary, the jobs apocalypse is not upon us. This isn't to say that changes aren't on the way, and that some may find their professions disrupted by new technologies very soon; but the proliferation of artificial intelligence (AI) and smart automation should not be cause for alarm, let alone panic. In fact, as we will outline over the course of the next chapters, AI and smart automation might actually *help* human workers gain significant boosts in productivity and in the quality of their work, accelerate the completion of tasks, minimize risk, improve outcomes and perhaps even manage to achieve a healthier work–life balance than they are able to today. Before we get ahead of ourselves though, let's spend a few moments looking back on the history of human–machine partnerships to better understand how our relationship with machines has almost always ultimately resulted in *more* opportunity, a *higher* quality of life, *longer* lifespans, and the kind of progress that has cured some of humanity's deadliest diseases, allowed anyone with a pocket-sized device to send information instantaneously to pretty much anyone on the planet, and send robot rovers to Mars.

This isn't the part of the book where we talk about the 'invention' of fire, or the first wheel or the first hoe. We already know how humanity got here. The long daisy chain of innovation linking our primate ancestors first picking up a stick to scoop tasty termites out of a termite mound to the engineer who just figured out how to perfectly land an autonomous probe on a tumbling asteroid millions of miles from Earth is something we all understand. From fire to club to wheel to hoe to catapult to windmill to printing press to steam engine to combustion engines to computers to moon landings to 3D goggles, humans keep devising new and clever ways to solve complex engineering problems. Some focus on medical challenges, others on agricultural ones. Some spend entire careers working on designing the best possible surfboard while others spend their entire lives trying to solve mathematical problems. Some dedicate their lives to finding a cure to a disease that took one of their loved ones, while some invent ways of gaming financial markets to make better investment bets. Give us 30 minutes with a human being from anywhere in the world and from any point in time throughout human history, and we will come away with a list of problems they wish someone with the wit, skills and tools would come along and fix. More often than not, that person will probably volunteer to do it themselves if only someone with the resources they need would just come along and give them a little help.

As a species, we solve problems. That's what we do. We didn't evolve an opposable thumb because we needed it to swing from branches. We evolved an opposable thumb because we manipulate objects with precision while we solve problems in the imperfect world around us. Put a human anywhere in the world, and they will build a shelter, make a tool, fabricate a trap, dig a well, and eventually customize their environment to be more comfortable, safer and more efficient than it was when they first landed there.

Now, consider the usefulness of a stick. A skinny stick can be used to pluck moisture out of a narrow crack in a rock. A thicker stick can be used as a club, or as a structural support for a shelter, or as a rudimentary digging instrument, or as part of a basic machine like an irrigation system, or a river boat or a lever. A stick is versatile, but it is essentially a physical extension of a human user's will: an attachment. A hand tool to lift, dig, break, reach, crush, hold, direct, pull or push. A stick isn't going to help a human being cure polio or stop the polar ice caps from melting. For its thousands of different uses, a stick is just a stick. The inexhaustible nature of human ingenuity notwithstanding, a stick has its limitations. In the same vein, a steam engine has its limitations. A steam engine can be used to irrigate fields, power assembly plants, propel freight trains across continents and ships across oceans, generate electricity for entire neighbourhoods, purify drinking water, manufacture medicines, transform cotton into fabrics – and on and on and on. Tools are tools. Tools are invented by humans to solve problems that they are not able to

Humans cannot succeed as a species without enhancements.

solve on their own. Why? Because humans are able to see beyond their own limitations and devise ways to overcome them. Human ingenuity isn't just about being clever. Human ingenuity is, first and foremost, born out of the realization that humans cannot succeed as a species without enhancements.

Let's look beyond sticks and steam engines for a moment. Shoes are tools too. Running shoes, rock-climbing shoes, ice-trekking shoes, cycling shoes, cowboy boots, soccer cleats and hundreds of other categories of specialized shoes are all tools – all *enhancements*. Every smart watch, steak knife, backpack, laptop, protein shake, keychain, light bulb, car tyre, toothbrush and microfiber shirt is a tool – an enhancement. We surround ourselves with the means to enhance our capabilities: to run faster, to throw further, to fly higher, to hit that ball over the net just a little bit harder than we did yesterday, to get that report finished just a little more quickly, to make that new investment yield better ROI than the one before it. Even the least ambitious among us are driven to improve ourselves and the world around us, if nothing else than by finding ways of working less to achieve the same results. Even when improving outcomes isn't our goal, we humans will find ways of doing things ever more efficiently. We are compelled to enhance ourselves and the environments we evolve in to simplify our lives and make everything we touch work for us instead of settling for the opposite.

This is true of dwellings as well. From the moment the first caveman decorated his first wall with hand prints and hunting scenes, human beings have been improving, customizing and enhancing their own environments in attempts to make them more useful. Human dwellings are filled with enhancements: in their most basic forms, they provide food storage, shelter from the elements, a place to store medicines, barriers against threats, comfortable bedding, a place to keep tools and treasure, a place to spend time with loved ones, and more often than not a place to prepare and cook food. The world's most advanced dwellings provide a place to store and recharge vehicles, work, relax, explore the world virtually, throw parties, recover from surgery, train for an athletic competition, earn a PhD, build rockets, do genetic research, build billion-dollar empires, write the next Great American Novel, or have every one of our wants and needs met by machines and specialized workers. Regardless of whether we live in a hand-built hut in the middle of nowhere or in the world's most technologically advanced super-smart-home, dwellings too are monuments to the human need to turn everything we touch into a tool – an *enhancement* of some kind.

The new technology revolution currently underway is no different: humans are simply finding better and more clever ways of enhancing themselves and their environments. The objective isn't to replace humans or to displace them, but to build new tools with which to do things faster, better, with less effort, and ideally at a lower cost.

Smart automation: a new pivot

What seems to be different about this new wave of technology advancements is the fact that they can think and mimic tasks that until now had been reserved for humans. A stick can't think or solve problems. Neither can a steam engine. Until recently, even when a machine was clever enough to pull its own levers, a human being still had to make all of its decisions for it: when to turn it on, when to turn it off, when to make adjustments to it, when to recalibrate it, when to upgrade it, when to apply it to one task instead of another. Machines were instruments. Humans maintained their control over them, and in so doing, over their own agency.

Suddenly, machines can make decisions for themselves. They know when to turn themselves on and off. They can make adjustments to themselves on their own, know when to recalibrate themselves, know when to update their software, know when to order replacement parts or maintenance. A human no longer has to stand there to pull levers, push buttons, turn off the lights at the end of the last shift. Increasingly, machines no longer need us as much as they used to, and that changes the equation somewhat. The relationship between human and machine is no longer purely that of *user* and *instrument*, but rather one of *user* and *helper*.

Never in recorded human history had this happened before. This is something new for humans to adjust to, and, aside from science fiction stories, they have no precedent to draw from. It is one thing to be entertained by the idea that robots will some day co-exist with humans and serve them. It is another altogether to suddenly find yourself confronted with the reality of a world increasingly shifting towards artificial intelligence, robots and automation handling tasks that humans depend on being to perform in order to collect a pay cheque. The science fiction implications of mining robots or firefighting robots taking over from humans is likely to focus on the benefits of that automation: sending robots to do dangerous jobs will save lives. No human being will ever have to die in a mine or fighting a fire ever again. The real-world implications of that innovative humanitarian improvement is that firefighters and miners will now find themselves without a job, or an income or economic prospects. How will those miners and firefighters put food on the table once their jobs have been taken over by machines? What will they have to show for their careers, for their hard work, for their courage, for their accomplishments? How will they continue to feel valuable to society, and contribute through hard work, skill and perseverance when their profession and identity have been taken away from them? Economic challenges aren't the only dimension to this displacement. A sense of purpose, identity and place also disappear when those jobs do. Pride and hope should also not be casualties of automation.

Now expand that scenario to every profession. Warehouse worker. Accountant. Assembly worker. Attorney. Fighter pilot.

Physician. Salesperson. Customer service representative. Executive assistant. Truck driver. Librarian. Bartender. Fry cook. Dishwasher. Farmhand. Border patrol agent. Architect. Engineer. Fire control officer. Recruiter. Advertising copywriter. Graphic artist. Journalist. Business analyst. Financial advisor. Whatever your job is, it can be automated. It is only a matter of time before someone builds the right combination of AI, machine learning, robotics, automation, sensors and data connectivity to be able to do what you do, only better and faster. The future we are beginning to glimpse is very much a future in which machines, which were once our instruments, and more recently our helpers, may become our replacements. That is the fear, at least. And for scores of workers throughout the world, the last few decades have shown the degree to which automation can transform industries and economies.

Understanding the impact of automation on employment

We only have to look at the transformation of the employment ecosystem in the United States in the last two centuries to see the effect that technology shifts can have on employment. For instance, the agricultural share of employment in the United States between 1850 to 1970 (essentially spanning the full breadth of industrialization in the United States from its start to its peak), dropped from roughly 60 per cent down to less than 5 per cent.[1] Similarly, since automation and globalization began to transform manufacturing, manufacturing's share of US employment shrank from 25 per cent in 1960 to less than 10 per cent today.[2] The more time you spend with this data, the more justification there may be in expressing concern about a possible automation apocalypse.

This seems as good a time as any to bring our discussion back from hypothetical scenarios to observable patterns from which we might derive valuable insights. We're going to start with this:

7

If humans weren't particularly concerned about being replaced by machines when they were merely tools, instruments and even helpers, then we can infer that as long as machines are meant to behave as tools, instruments and helpers, they do not present a threat to human employment.

Their role, as such, is to assist and enhance, not replace. This teaches us that not all automation is threatening to human employment. Only the types of automation designed to replace humans, and actually *capable* of replacing humans, represent a legitimate threat to employment. Every other kind of automation – automation designed to assist and enhance humans in various tasks – is therefore *not* a threat to employment. This means that when we speak *generally* about automation, without differentiating between enhancement tools and replacement tools, we may be exaggerating the degree to which automation as a whole poses a threat.

Humans are also used to working in partnership with non-human helpers. We have been doing this for thousands of years. Humans and dogs hunt together. Humans work with dogs to herd and protect livestock. Humans and oxen work together to till fields and pull heavy loads. Mules and horses help carry loads, pull carriages and carry riders on their backs. Humans have trained falcons to hunt, geese to act as early warning systems, and pigeons to carry messages. Humans throughout the world partner with animals to grow food, power machinery, transport goods, guard their homes, keep grain storage rodent-free and explore new frontiers. Where would humanity be without its partnerships with bees, dogs, cats, horses, cows, elephants and silk worms? Our point here is to remind you that humans don't limit their pursuit of enhancement and augmentation to tools and machines. Conscious, intelligent, living beings also play into humanity's innovation ecosystem. Humans have successfully partnered with a variety of intelligent helpers for thousands of years. Again, with little fear of being replaced by dogs, horses and bees, these types of partnerships evolved and prospered without great incident. Only in science fiction have we explored the possibility that humans might be replaced by super-intelligent animals, from George Orwell's allegorical *Animal Farm* to Pierre Boulle's more apocalyptic *La Planète des Singes*.[3,4]

Humans are therefore no strangers to partnering with intelligent, sentient tools. What is a living being, after all, if not an organic machine? What is a service machine if not a mechanical service animal? Are service animals and machines not trained to obey certain commands, perform specific tasks, and enhance the capabilities of their human masters? Once you realize that partnering with an intelligent mechanical tool has more in common with partnering with a service animal than with entering into an unholy bargain with one of our future 'robot overlords', the threat of robots taking over becomes far less terrifying.

> *Humans are no strangers to partnering with intelligent, sentient tools.*

Reminder: real-world AI is not movie AI

It is also worth bringing up that most artificial intelligence is not all that evolved, and will not be for some time. Artificial Intelligence – or AI for short – is still, for the most part, both misunderstood and overhyped. While some experimental AI projects like IBM's Watson and Google's Deep Mind already test the limits of human-like machine intelligence (or rather, machine intelligence that can *mimic* human intelligence), the vast majority of AI products and use cases have absolutely nothing to do with the general public's perception of 'AI'. Most AI is not Watson, let alone *2001: A Space Odyssey*'s Hal 9000 onboard computer, or Tony Stark's J.A.R.V.I.S. or *Knight Rider*'s talking car (K.I.T.T.).[5,6,7]

Most AI is limited to very narrow types of tasks, from machine vision in smartphone cameras and noise cancellation capabilities in smart speakers to driver-assist emergency braking in passenger cars. The human-like intelligent AI that we have all marvelled at in movies and TV shows is not coming for your job. The kind of smart automation that technology experts and pundits talk about when they discuss the future of jobs is *not* that. It is, in many ways, the same kind of smart automation that allows your phone to speed-dial your spouse at a simple voice command, or to regulate your home's temperature while you sleep, or to monitor your bank account for suspicious activity. Teaching machines to perform tasks that humans find value in delegating should not be threatening to anyone, and these tasks, currently, represent many of the tasks being automated.

An example: how might smart automation in transportation affect professional drivers?

Consider the sorts of onboard AIs being developed for autonomous vehicles. Ignore where the technology is today, and project yourself into a future when truly autonomous vehicles will be a mature technology. What will self-driving cars really be able to do? Simple: they will allow drivers to delegate the operation of their vehicle to the vehicle's onboard AI. These cars will park themselves, drive their owners around, avoid accidents, reroute themselves around traffic jams, and even run errands for their owners while they are at work. Wonderful stuff. But the worry is that this kind of autonomous functionality will eliminate the need for professional drivers. Is that a fair concern? The simple answer is yes: it *is* a fair concern. We would caution, however, that it may ultimately be overhyped.

For starters, since most households do not employ personal drivers, adding autonomous driving to personal vehicles will not displace the vast majority of for-hire drivers currently on the roads today.

Now let us address the threat that this poses to *professional* drivers (taxi drivers, delivery drivers, public transportation drivers and commercial truck drivers). According to the United States Department of Labor Statistics, there were roughly 305,000 licensed hired car drivers, 1,421,000 delivery truck drivers, nearly 2 million commercial 'big rig' truck drivers, and 687,000 bus drivers in the United States in 2016.[8] That's a total of 4.5 million drivers who could find themselves affected by the arrival of fully autonomous vehicles.

First things first: the arrival of fully autonomous vehicles isn't going to be sudden. If it happens, it will happen over time, in successive waves of technology improvements and implementations that will allow every affected industry to adjust expectations, plan for coming changes and adapt.

Secondly, legislation and regulation will create additional roadblocks to the proliferation of autonomous vehicle technology into commercial sectors. Countries, states, and municipalities will need to adjust their laws to protect the public and address the scores of new challenges that autonomous vehicles will bring to our roadways. New zoning ordinances will have to be devised, with autonomous and no-autonomous driving zones almost certainly among the defining features of the transition period during which the market matures.

Thirdly, massive infrastructure improvements will be needed to assist autonomous vehicles in environments shared by cyclists, pedestrians and human-driven vehicles. Some of these infrastructure investments will manifest themselves as special-use lanes and physical barriers, but many will also be technology investments whose purpose will be to help manage V2I (vehicle to infrastructure) and V2P (vehicle to pedestrian) interactions. Their development, approval and installation will not scale overnight either. Also, don't forget to factor in labour and trade unions, which also may delay and even outright block the automation of commercial driving. In other words, even if automakers are already testing autonomous 18-wheelers, delivery vans and passenger vehicles on major highways and controlled urban environments, it will be years (and perhaps decades) before commercial drivers truly run the risk of being displaced at scale by autonomous vehicles.

Moreover, driving the vehicle is only one aspect of being a commercial driver. Trucks also have to be loaded and unloaded. Delivery drivers have to pick up and deliver parcels. Taxi and limo drivers often have to assist their fares with luggage, to say nothing of the expectation of friendliness and service. Public transportation drivers also often assist passengers, tourists and pedestrians in distress in addition to driving their buses and trams. To distil every value-added task performed by a commercial driver down to just driving a vehicle from Point A to Point B is fundamentally to misunderstand what being a commercial driver entails.

Task automation vs *job* automation: a key to understanding the future of human–machine partnerships

This brings us to an observation that we will come back to more than once in this book: while most *tasks* can be automated, most *jobs* cannot. The *task* of driving is different from the *job* of being a driver. The *task* of searching for a known terrorist's face in a crowd is different from the *job* of being a counterterrorism agent. The *task* of looking through 50,000 pages of financial documents for errors is different from the *job* of being an accountant. Tasks are not jobs. Only when jobs are limited to only a handful of tasks (or just one repetitive task) can they be automated. The more complex the job, and the more tasks it involves, the more difficult it is to be automated.

While most tasks *can be automated, most* jobs *cannot.*

Once you start to make a list of all of the tasks performed by various commercial drivers during the course of their work, you begin to realize that the introduction of autonomous vehicles into their professional equation doesn't come close to addressing other driving-adjacent tasks. When it comes to delivery drivers especially, for all the media attention around flying drone deliveries and delivery robots, the reality is that no robot or drone realistically threatens to displace delivery drivers. Drones can fall out of the sky, get tangled up in trees and utility lines, get shot down, stolen, vandalized and hacked, plunge into bodies of water, and get blown off course by weather. Delivery robots can be stolen, vandalized, robbed, hacked, kicked, run over by a vehicle, washed away in a flood, and damaged by weather. For reasons that still baffle many technology observers, robots are also often the victims of unprovoked violence. This might be a humorous parenthesis in our discussion if it did not underline a possible grave obstacle to human–machine partnerships – one that could grow into a much more widespread problem than it is today. For now, the issue of random attacks on robots is mostly a practical cost-accounting matter, however: If enough delivery robots are routinely molested or vandalized while making their deliveries, at what point does it become counterproductive to entrust deliveries to robots?

Fact: no robot can currently make pickups and deliveries as quickly and reliably as a human being. The driving aspect of deliveries can be automated, much like parcel-tracking and route-planning can be automated, but first yard and last yard tasks (the physical pickups and deliveries) cannot be. Not in any way that would make financial or operational sense, at any rate.

It is far more likely that vehicle automation will bring *changes* to commercial driving jobs rather than the job apocalypse so many fear will. Perhaps 'drivers' will no longer be drivers. That *is* possible. Perhaps their job titles will change to something new. Perhaps 'freight engineer' will replace today's 'truck driver'. Perhaps 'transportation agent' will some day replace 'bus driver'. Perhaps 'delivery specialist' will replace 'delivery driver'. The nomenclature isn't really important at this juncture. What *is* important is that it is far more likely that new technologies will *transform* many of the jobs that the public worries about perhaps losing to automation than that automation will *eliminate* them altogether. Driving, after all, is just a task. Creating machines that drive for us when we need them to isn't an act of destruction. Creating machines that drive for us when we need them to is an act of augmentation. Autonomous vehicles aren't designed to replace us. They are designed to *enhance* us.

New tools, enhancements and human–machine partnerships: what to expect next

What we can infer from this broad example is that our appreciation of the value and role that automation yet have to play in human evolution may have jumped the rails. As tedious, dangerous and uncomfortable tasks find themselves increasingly automated, and as human need for computational, analytical and predictive power increases exponentially, what we observe is little more than the same application of innovation, ingenuity and wit once assigned to simpler problems now being assigned to new sets of problems. While the difficulty of the problems increases with every next advance in human engineering, the problem-solving spirit that fuels invention has not changed. The objective, as always, is not to *replace* humans but to *enhance* humans.

Every generation of invention in human history was followed by a period of adaptation. Hunters learned to be farmers. Farmers learned to be sailors. Sailors learned to be traders. Traders learned to be bankers. 19th-century artisans became 20th-century factory workers, and 20th-century factory workers became 21st-century information workers. Innovation triggers adaptations. Hard labour progressively makes way to soft labour. What used to be backbreaking work no longer needs to be backbreaking because human beings, despite their capacity for grit, always dream up better, less painful ways of getting work done. And what we observe, in almost every instance of technological and labour evolution, is that the workers fastest to adapt to change and transition into new professions always reap the rewards of that agility and initiative. Those slowest to adapt, along with those who refuse to, get stuck in occupations that become less competitive and provide fewer career opportunities. Farmers didn't vanish when workers moved to the city to work in factories. The nature of farming just changed. Labour is adaptable in the same way that humanity is adaptable, and if humanity is anything, aside from ingenious, it *is* adaptable.

One of the ways that we believe automation will transform jobs – or rather *occupations* – is by automating so many tasks that used to take a team of people to accomplish. In that manner, several adjacent or interdependent roles could see themselves consolidated into one. A simple example of this is a two-person executive and an executive assistant 'team'. Because many of the tasks once handled by an executive assistant can now be managed by digital assistants and AIs – from answering phones and managing schedules to setting appointments and drafting memos – a business executive capable of making their own espresso could easily manage to go about their day with digital assistants and AIs.

So, what happens to human assistants in this kind of scenario? If the assistants are any good, they get recommended for other positions somewhere in the company, and earn themselves a promotion and a raise. If they aren't any good, they have a choice: either become an executive assistant at a less technologically forward company, or look for another kind of job altogether. Executive assistant jobs will never completely disappear for the same reason that limousine driver jobs will never completely disappear. Individuals who can afford the personal touch of having a human do a job that a machine could do will always prefer the premium option of employing human staff.

We believe that task consolidation through smart automation will *transform* jobs more than kill them, and shift more workers into other roles than it sends to the unemployment rolls.

Having said that, the fact remains that in a job consolidation model, displaced workers have to find somewhere to go and something new to do. That is a friction point that we will now look at.

Smart automation and job consolidation: who is most at risk?

The problem with finding data and data-driven predictions about the upcoming jobs apocalypse isn't that there isn't enough of it, but rather that there is too much of it. Consequently, a significant percentage of it is derivative, and the vast majority of it is dubious at best. Irony of ironies: sifting through study after study, looking for data and methodologies that we found credible (or data sets large enough to be relevant) was an excruciating exercise we wish we could have handed over to a team of AIs. Sadly, we aren't quite living in the future yet, and we had to do this research work by hand. We did manage, over the course of nearly eight months of research, to narrow down our list of reports and studies to a half dozen that we felt were on the right track. We're going to look at several of their findings, specifically with regard to which job categories and professions are currently most at risk of being displaced by automation.

In Brooking's 2019 *Automation and Artificial Intelligence: How machines are affecting people and places*, Mark Muro, Robert Maxim and Jacob Whiton note that 1 in 4 US jobs (roughly 36 million jobs) is *highly* susceptible to automation.[9] An additional 36 per cent (roughly 52 million jobs) find themselves at medium risk of being automated. The remaining 39 per cent (57 million jobs) have a very low risk of being automated. We interpret this as more of a feature of successive future waves of automation than as a fixed analysis about the automation potential of jobs. What we mean by this is that we see these numbers as meaning that 36 million jobs are at high risk of being automated in the next decade, another 52 million jobs will be at high risk of being automated in the decade after that, followed by another 57 million jobs following suit in the decade following that one. (We are rounding the timeframes down to decades for clarity.)

The report also points out that the lowest wage jobs are the most exposed to automation. In other words, the 36 million US jobs currently at risk of being automated tend to be low wage jobs, and the progression to the next batch of jobs, and the one after that, will roughly follow an upward-income trajectory, with the lowest wage jobs being automated first, and the highest wage jobs being automated last. These are generalizations, but the trend seems to hold true, as it always has: landowners, factory owners, newspaper moguls are usually the last to find themselves displaced or financially stressed by technological innovation. It is usually the lowest wage earners who are displaced and challenged first.

Notable exceptions can be expected, however. For instance, maintenance technicians and janitorial staff are unlikely to be replaced by machines any time soon, as most buildings are not designed to be maintained and cleaned by robots, and robots are not yet versatile or dependable enough to be able to get into all of the tight places that humans can. Hairdressers and cosmetologists, many of whom are not among the highest earners, are also unlikely to be replaced by machines any time soon. The same can be said of waiting staff, auto mechanics and landscaping workers.

The study lists two dozen job categories in order of risk, and the breakdown essentially boils down to this: foodservice, production, office and administrative support, farming/fishing/forestry, transportation and material moving, construction and extraction, and installation/maintenance/repair appear to round out the most high-risk occupations.

The next batch of occupations at risk of being replaced (or at least severely affected by automation) are: sales, healthcare support, legal, computer and mathematical, protection services and personal care.

Lastly, at the bottom of the risk list come healthcare practitioners and technicians, life sciences, management, arts/entertainment/sports/media, architecture and engineering, education, business and financial operations.

We would caution that a number of financial operations occupations may be at much higher risk of automation than forestry jobs, but in general, this study from Brookings is consistent with our own observations.

In PwC's *Will Robots Really Steal Our Jobs?* report, John Hawksworth, Richard Berriman and Goel Saloni shine additional light on the subject.[10] Their insight into the role that successive waves of job automation might have over human employment over time echoes our view. They suggest three successive waves stretching into the 2030s:

- an *algorithmic wave*, in which 'automation of simple tasks and analysis of structured data' will impact mostly data-driven sectors;
- an *augmentation wave*, in which 'dynamic interactions with technology for clerical support and decision-making', along with 'robotic tasks in semi-controlled environments' (geofenced areas like manufacturing plants and warehouses), will expand automation into more complex and traditionally human-driven tasks;
- and an *autonomous wave*, in which 'automation of physical labour and manual dexterity', alongside 'problem-solving in dynamic real-world situations that require responsive actions' will further expand automation into areas that had until then been the privy of highly specialized, intelligent, collaborative beings.

In their study, industries considered most at risk of being transformed by automation during the first wave are (in order of highest to lowest risk): financial and insurance, professional/scientific/technical, and information and communication/public administration and defence. Note that PwC expects that no job category on this list will see more than a 10 per cent rate of automation in that first wave.

Industries considered most at risk of being transformed by automation during the second wave include all of the above, only nearer a 20 per cent rate of automation, with the addition of transportation and storage, manufacturing, construction, administrative and support services, wholesale and retail trade, foodservice, and human health and social work.

Lastly, the third wave of automation predicted by PwC is expected to wreak the most havoc on transportation and storage, construction, manufacturing, administrative and support services, wholesale and retail trade, and foodservice.

Note that of all the industries studied, the category that fared best was education, with less than 10 per cent risk of automation after all three waves. Another point of note is that only one industry reached a 50 per cent risk of severe disruption after all three waves: transportation and storage. All others were below 50 per cent.

Based on PwC's projections, the impact of automation on the above industries over time also appears to level off in the first half of the 2030s, suggesting that automation may only displace a portion of the human workforce rather than the majority of it. Some job categories may not fare all that well, however. Digging deeper still into PwC's study, we found that the jobs most at risk of being automated in the next two decades are:

- machine operators and assemblers (60–70 per cent);
- clerical workers (50–60 per cent);
- elementary occupations (40–55 per cent);
- crafts and related trades (40–50 per cent);
- technicians and associated professionals (25–35 per cent);
- service and sales workers (25–35 per cent).

Below this one-third threshold of automation risk, we find skilled agricultural and fishery workers (15–30 per cent), professionals (10 per cent), and senior officials and managers (5–10 per cent).

Here is where PwC's data provides insight into one of the reasons why some occupations are more vulnerable to automation than others. The study compares machine operators and assemblers (the most at-risk category) and professionals (the second least vulnerable category) based on six categories of tasks and skills they are expected to utilize in their day-to-day responsibilities: manual tasks, routine tasks, computation, management, social skills and literacy skills. Compared to the average of all occupations, what the data reveals is that machine operators and assemblers are 168 per cent more dependent on manual tasks than other human workers, while professionals' task composition puts their manual tasks at 48 per cent of the average. Similarly, machine operators and assemblers' task composition puts routine tasks at 124 per cent higher than the average while professionals fall at 93 per cent of the average. In computation, however, machine operators and assemblers fall at 51 per cent of the average while professionals find themselves at 142 per cent of the average. With regard to management skills, the difference is 84 per cent against 92 per cent. What does this tell us?

Automation is a game of tasks, not a game of occupations.

- First, it tells us that automation is a game of tasks, not a game of occupations. For a machine operator, the obvious target of automation will be any area in which his or her task accounts for an above average amount of time – in this instance manual tasks and routine tasks. For our professional, computation tasks will likely be the first target of automation. What we see here is that efficiency improvements by way of automation can just as easily find their way into an occupation at a low risk of being automated as they can into an occupation considered at high risk of being automated.

- Secondly, it reveals that even machine operator and assembly occupations require skills and tasks comparable to those of allegedly less automatable 'professionals.' For instance, machine operators and assemblers' 84 per cent of average score with regard to management tasks isn't all that far removed from professionals' 92 per cent of the average. In other words, just because some tasks can easily be automated doesn't mean that the entire job can – or should – be. If machine operators' and assemblers' task composition with regard to management responsibilities is almost identical to that of other professionals, this tells us that certain important aspects of their job may be overlooked by proponents of automation. Caution ahead, as they overlook these responsibilities at their own peril. Oversimplifying what human jobs actually entail in the real world and relying perhaps too much on written job descriptions may not ultimately be the most effective way of making real-world decisions about efficiency and outcome improvement.

Automation as a means of *increasing* human potential: which traits and skills will automation help promote in human workers?

We again argue that automation will not replace jobs outright but augment and enhance them by streamlining and simplifying certain repetitive or low-value tasks. In the case of the machine operator, manual-labour and routine tasks are most likely to be automated, while management, team-building, employee training and production supervision may now find themselves moved into priority roles. Likewise, our professional's routine and computational tasks may find themselves automated, making room for other priorities like management, employee development and technology upskilling.

When used properly, automation doesn't kill jobs, it rearranges their structure. And in the most outcome-driven scenarios, it *improves* their structure by creating *more* opportunities for human workers to focus on high-value tasks that cannot be automated.

Another way to look at automation is as a time-creation engine: automation manufactures time. Every man-hour it takes on is a man-hour gained. That man-hour can be subtracted from a company's balance sheet and treated as a cost savings, or it can be reassigned to a high-value task that could not, until then, be budgeted for. Thus, each man-hour assigned to a machine creates an additional man-hour that can be assigned to a capable, high-value human worker. When we mentioned that automation should be additive rather than subtractive earlier in the chapter, this is what we meant: a hundred man-hour hours freed by an effective use of automation could be treated as a cost saving, but doesn't it make more sense to maximize the value of that gain in one hundred man-hours, and reinvest it in the company? Apply it to solving a problem, improving a system, building a new revenue stream, designing the next killer app?

The lowest hanging fruit in the business world is finding ways to cut costs. This isn't to say that running a lean organization doesn't have its advantages. Cutting costs and trimming fat in ways that ultimately help companies perform better are always wins. But the reflex to cut costs just because you can isn't necessarily the best way to drive towards market leadership. Sometimes, re-tasking resources from low-value to high-value tasks makes more sense than throwing them away.

A case in point: digital transformation, technology disruption, and the monumental task of rebuilding businesses for a 21st-century digital economy are not the types of challenges that companies can hope to address successfully by cutting costs and cutting corners. Smart, agile companies know how to unlock their own parts and move them around at will. They are modular. Job descriptions and departments evolve. IT managers at these companies aren't operating the way they were 10 years ago or 5 years ago, or even a year ago. Every aspect of the business is in a state of constant change and adaptation. Automation for these types of companies, which are typically digital leaders, isn't used to shrink the number of employees. It is used to free up capital to hire more people, and free up human workers to focus on more high-value and meaningful tasks.

Shifting human capital from low-value tasks to high-value tasks

So what are the types of high-value tasks that automation will help humans focus on more? Which skills and traits will emerge from an increasingly automated economy as most valuable to employers, collaborators and investors? Which skills and traits should today's workers start developing now in order to attract tomorrow's recruiters?

In its March 2018 *Automation, Skills, and Training* report, the OECD (Organization for Economic Co-operation and Development) provides insight into the relationship between various occupational qualifications and the risk of automation.[11] Based on data from a 2012 employment survey, Ljubica Nedelkoska and Glenda Quintini note that creative intelligence and social intelligence skills may be significantly less automatable than perception and manipulation skills, meaning that human workers displaying high degrees of creative intelligence, social intelligence, and skilled in non-routine interactive and cognitive tasks, are most likely to be valued by employers, regardless of automation.

Conversely, workers whose occupations are heavily rooted in routine or manual tasks find themselves most at risk of being displaced by automation. Manual skills, for all their specialized value, are simply likely to find increasingly niche value among tomorrow's employers. Again, we do not predict an apocalypse of skilled manual jobs, but rather an erosion of somewhere between one-third and half of all manual jobs combined. Machine operators and assembly workers are more likely to feel the bite of automation than other skilled manual labour (like hairdressers and computer repair specialists, for example), so beware generalizations relating to the automation of manual labour as a whole.

Referencing data provided by the World Economic Forum, Nedelkoska and Quintini highlight the shift in global top high-demand skills between 2015 and 2020 by providing us with two lists.

The 2015 list:

1 complex problem-solving;
2 coordination with others;
3 people management;
4 critical thinking;
5 negotiation;
6 quality control;
7 service orientation;
8 judgement and decision-making;
9 active listening;
10 creativity.

The 2020 list:

1 complex problem-solving;
2 critical thinking;
3 creativity;
4 people management;
5 coordination with others;
6 emotional intelligence;
7 judgement and decision-making;
8 service orientation;
9 negotiation;
10 cognitive flexibility.

Note the addition of emotional intelligence to the list and the disappearance of quality control (an automatable task). Bear in mind that complex problem-solving, critical thinking, creativity, people management, emotional intelligence, judgement, service orientation, negotiation and cognitive flexibility are all applications of high-level cognitive and interactive skillsets.

In another five years we expect to see complex problem-solving, people management, coordination/collaboration, service orientation and decision-making to move down the list. Why? Because these skills can and will be augmented by artificial intelligence and smart automation.

The remaining traits – critical thinking, judgement, emotional intelligence, creativity and cognitive flexibility – should move to the top five spots for non-automatable, high-value, sought-after human skills most prized by employers.

Human–machine partnerships as an intuitive and balanced evolutionary response to smart automation

Before we focus on how to adapt to the rise of automation and AI and consider the kinds of changes that are on the way, and which types of occupations will most likely find themselves enhanced and improved by it all, let us take a moment to circle back to the start.

Fact: human ingenuity and innovation have always been about improving performance, about enhancing and augmenting human capabilities, about increasing output, strength, speed, range, strength, power, efficiency, effectiveness, yield and opportunities. Humanity is at its best when it uses the tools and stratagems of its own making as means to do more, or to free itself from the constraints of tedious tasks in order to be able to do more.

Thus, the farmer who turns to artificial intelligence and the Internet of Things (IoT) to help him work his farm isn't all that different from the farmer who, long ago, built a mechanical irrigation system for his fields, and used the river at the edge of his farm to power his mill. Likewise, the attorney who turns to machine learning and artificial intelligence to look for errors or mentions of specific individuals or contradictory statements through thousands of pages of court documents and depositions isn't all that different from the lawyer who, long ago, had to call upon small armies of interns to do the same. Automating a process or a task does not mean that jobs have to die. It only means that jobs have to change.

Now, as machines become not only more sophisticated and autonomous but intelligent, and as machines become capable of learning skills and making basic decisions, our relationship is beginning to change. Users, drivers, and the role of the operator (or *user*) is evolving into something else – something more akin to the types of partnerships that humans have formed with animal helpers over the millennia. And as intelligent machines gain the ability to interact with humans as if they were themselves human – using natural language, human-like voices and through casual social interactions – these partnerships will increasingly become more akin to the types of partnerships that humans form with one another.

Thus, the owner of an autonomous driving car may soon be able to partner with his vehicle to commute to work, run errands during the day, perhaps generate a little revenue by picking up and dropping off pedestrians in need of a ride, pick up a family member from the airport, or go out to collect a bowl of chicken soup when he is too sick to leave the house. At the office, a business manager will soon be able to create multitasking teams of specialized AIs tasked with performing a plethora of useful tasks, from generating reports, providing market analysis and creating presentations to coordinating with her human teammates, organizing her schedule and assisting her in making complex business-critical decisions. Even manual-labour occupations, from landscapers to machine operators, will soon be able to partner with AIs, robots and smart automation

Automation doesn't have to be a job Armageddon.

tools to work faster, better, and be free to do more than yester-day's technologies allowed them to. Automation doesn't have to be a job Armageddon. In fact, it shouldn't be. The economic and innovation potential to be derived from human–machine part-nerships is far more interesting and full of opportunity than an alternative in which automation is wasted on cutting corners, cutting costs and ignoring the lessons of the last three billion years of human evolution and progress.

CHAPTER TWO

The state of human–machine partnerships

Evaluating human–machine partnerships: the importance of finding common ground

So that we can get a useful and practical understanding of human–machine partnerships, we must have a way of evaluating them. But how?

There are many ways of doing this. For instance, we can look at where certain categories of human–machine partnerships fall on a spectrum of societal, economic and political needs. We can take a classical business approach and use the tried-and-true SWOT analysis model to evaluate human–machine relationships based on their strengths, weaknesses, opportunities and threats. We can take a simple binary approach: valuable vs not valuable; harmful vs beneficial; expensive vs cheap; necessary vs frivolous; scalable vs niche; easy vs difficult; valuable vs not valuable; and so on. But with so many different ways of thinking about human–machine partnerships, how can we have a consistent evaluation model that consumers, developers, academics, business decision-makers and policy decision-makers agree on? How do we find common ground?

The most obvious variable here is the *context* of the evaluation, or put another way, the *purpose* behind it. A social scientist, for instance, will probably not seek to evaluate a particular category of human–machine partnership in the same way that a chief logistics officer at a Fortune 100 company will seek to evaluate it. The former may be interested in the impact that a particular category of human–machine partnership may have on employment (or, more to the point, *un*employment), poverty, crime and so on. The latter may be interested mostly in evaluating that same human–machine partnership based on its impact on operational efficiency and speed to market, and/or its internal cost reduction potential, with little or no concern for its socio-economic ripple effects beyond the boundary of the company's outermost parking lot.

Here is the crux of the problem when it comes to thinking about human–machine partnerships: depending on the person performing the evaluation, the intent, evaluating equations and conclusions, become infinitely variable. (Depending on an individual's role, purpose, operational line of sight and the unique set of biases that ultimately frame his or her judgement, the result of the evaluation of a human–machine partnership may vary.) Value, like beauty, tends to lie in the eye of the beholder. This is no different: the value of a human–machine partnership will almost always be somewhat subjective.

To get around this hurdle, let's go back basics, and what we may want to call intuitive ROI: cost vs benefit. The most natural way to begin evaluating any category of human–machine partnership is perhaps to gauge whether its benefits outweigh its costs. Once we have established that, we can go from there.

As we already discussed, a social scientist and a corporate executive will have very different views of what benefits and costs matter in their valuation – but that's all right. What matters is that, regardless of role, purpose, operational line of sight and individual biases, the core methodology remains the same: *Do the benefits of this category of human–machine partnership outweigh its costs?* Having corporate executives and social scientists perform the same type of evaluation from their own unique perspectives is a good thing, and here are two reasons why.

On the one hand, by sharing their unique data sets and insights with one another, both groups can help flag and outline additional opportunities, risks and pain points that may not have otherwise turned up on everyone's radar. A socially responsible company, for instance, might be interested to learn that while the impact of deploying a particular category of human–machine partnership would greatly improve its operational efficiency and profitability, its downside might be layoffs, the dehumanization of customer experiences, and the possibility of a PR crisis that may snowball into damage to the company's reputation with consumers. What we find here is that by helping different groups or teams with very different interests and perspectives answer the same question, they can all contribute to one another's evaluation of a new technology or category of human–machine partnership.

Whether you are a cost accountant, a CEO, a social scientist, an economist, a crisis management strategist, a city planner, a technology analyst or a political pollster, benefiting from a common language *and* a common evaluation scheme makes debate, collaboration and joint analysis infinitely more probable and effective than unilateral and entirely subjective alternatives. Establishing that common ground and a common language as well are good next steps in our process of evaluation.

Evaluating human–machine partnerships: from cost–benefit thinking to cause-and-effect modelling

Now let's make this basic methodology a little more interesting. The question being asked here isn't so much one of *benefit vs cost* in the most literal sense of the term (as in the kind of maths typically found in an ROI equation), but one of *benefits vs consequences*. What businesses, governments and other entities studying the potential benefits and costs of investing in certain categories of human–machine partnerships should be asking themselves in addition to 'what will this cost, what are its potential benefits, and do the benefits outweigh the costs', are 'what are the potential consequences', and 'do the potential benefits outweigh the potential consequences?'

Adding this layer of evaluation to a standard cost–benefit analysis forces evaluators to think in terms of cause and effect rather than in terms of transactional maths. It helps them move from a balance sheet mode of thinking to a more forward-looking and organic analysis of what comes next. Why is this important?

Looking at a transformational initiative merely from a cost-accounting perspective is dangerous and myopic.

First, because looking at a transformational initiative like a new type of human–machine partnership merely from a cost-accounting perspective is dangerous and myopic. It doesn't account for real-world causality. Secondly, because the real costs and risks of signing off any transformative initiative lie in the types of changes that initiative will bring about *after* it has been set in motion; no organization can afford to be so reckless as to not consider or plan for likely consequences of their transformative initiatives.

For example, by helping elderly patients manage their own health from home, IoT and AI solutions can cut their healthcare costs in half while delivering round-the-clock monitoring, decreasing the risk of accidental drug overdoses, and allowing them to remain in their own homes rather than having to move to assisted-living facilities. However, having elderly patients partner with machines more than humans to manage their health could result in unintended consequences like a rise in depression and stress, which would obviously not improve their quality of life. Why? Because while intelligent homecare solutions may improve certain medical outcomes and make perfect sense from a cost–benefit angle, the simple act of replacing human care-givers with machines may rob patients of the human contact they need in their daily lives, and cannot do without. To help address this potential problem, toymaker Hasbro has jumped into the elder-care IoT space early with robotic pets to hopefully bridge the gap between robot companions and real pets.[1] This doesn't quite fix the problem, but it does help address and alleviate it. The National Science Foundation and researchers at Brown University have even partnered with Hasbro to add functionality and life-like behaviours to the robotic pets. More recently, Tombot partnered with Jim Henson's Creature Shop to create a very realistic robotic pup companion, so the need to make caretaker and companion robots feel and behave less artificial is already well ingrained in the design culture that will produce future generations of this technology.[2]

The above examples illustrate how thinking through consequences, not simply costs and potential benefits, can make all the difference in the world when it comes to implementing transformative new types of human–machine partnerships, and getting their design philosophy right. The same kind of thinking must be applied to all new types of human–machine partnerships, from education, healthcare and public safety, to customer service, social services, collaboration and manufacturing. Designing products, services and platforms that deliver benefits that vastly outweigh the cost of their implementation and deployment is ultimately just a matter of solving engineering problems and getting price points right. The real challenge, in our view, is for technology companies to anticipate potential ripples of unintended consequences caused by the introduction of their innovation into our everyday lives, and addressing them with intuitive design.

Here are a few types of ripples that technologists and product managers should always keep in the backs of their minds while designing their next generation of smart automation products:

- A progressive erosion of critical social skills among children educated in part by machines.
- The increased risk of data and privacy breaches in increasingly automated and datacentric healthcare systems.
- The danger to individual freedoms posed by public safety investments in smart technologies that could enable the rise of a surveillance-driven police state.
- The end of human employment in the customer service industry.
- Social erosion and increased emotional detachment between people and the institutions tasked with serving them.
- More efficient business collaboration may reduce friction so much that a reduction in the clash of competing ideas may result in a slower pace of innovation.
- A sharp decline in human employment in the manufacturing sector.

When it comes down to it, unintended consequences are costs, which is why it behooves us to learn to think of them as such. Here is a simple exercise to help product designers and product managers understand how this fits into technology design:

Question 1: What is the cost of doing (or not doing) X now?
Question 2: What will be the consequences of that choice later?
Question 3: Will it cost more or less to address that problem then instead of now?

Identifying solutions to address the possible consequences (ie *costs*) of technology design blind spots is just good business, if for no other reason than going through that process opens up entirely new areas of design and functionality possibility early in the innovation process. This can easily translate into a market advantage, as being the first-mover in a category doesn't always translate into long-term leadership. Being first *and* the best, however, is usually a winning combination. The ideal entrepreneurial model of problem-solving is not: see a problem, build a solution, monetize said solution. The ideal entrepreneurial model of problem-solving is: see a problem, build the right solution, minimize unintended consequences, monetize said solution. This forms the basis for the business justification of designing smart automation technologies that minimize unintended consequences and negative impact, not only on users and outcomes, but society and the economy as a whole.

This type of forethought-driven design highlights the importance of basing technology product evaluations, especially those that involve a potential for human–machine partnerships, on a broader value scale than the traditional cost–benefit analysis still favoured by cost accountants. Simply put, technology companies must learn to think more broadly about the meaning of costs and benefits as they relate to their innovation and problem-solving process. Companies that adapt quickly to this new reality will find themselves in a position to build better products with fewer pain points than those that either reject this model or struggle to adopt it.

Big Brother vs Big Mother vs Big Butler

One of the most perplexing challenges analysts have to deal with is how to make the complicated simple. With regard to understanding the opportunities, risks and threats of new technologies in general, we have devised a simple, instinctively relevant model of analysis to help us do just that.

Initially, we started with a simple binary model of 'friend vs foe' model of analysis, in which technologies that brought more unintended consequences than opportunity were qualified as 'foe', and technologies whose benefits outweighed negative side effects or abuse were qualified as 'friend'. As with all first versions of anything, that binary model was too limited, and we quickly began working on improving it. It wasn't long before we realized that technologies and how they are used naturally fall into three distinct categories, or *archetypes*: *Big Brother*, *Big Mother* and *Big Butler*.

One of the advantages of this trinity is that it is self-explanatory. Most people have been exposed to George Orwell's *1984*, or at the very least the myriad cultural references to one of its central entities, known as 'Big Brother'. And anyone familiar with the spectre of Big Brother will probably have a visceral understanding of the threat that entity represents to individual freedoms, privacy and personal security. How this applies to technology in the age of digital privacy, Big Data and the surveillance economy – in which technologies are used to track our activities and behaviours both online and offline – should be evident. 'Big Mother' refers to technologies that may be well intentioned but are perhaps overbearing and intrusive, like an overreaching, overzealous parent. Lastly, 'Big Butler' represents technologies that are entirely dedicated to serving human users, on their terms, with no intrusions, no breaches of privacy and very few pain points.

Big Butler is the ideal of the three technological archetypes.

Big Butler is the ideal of the three technological archetypes because it aims to strike the perfect balance between the benefits of smart automation, the management of data security (and user privacy), and an intuitively harmonious integration of smart technologies into our everyday lives. Big Butler is the precise opposite of Big Brother, and as such, the archetype that every smart technology should aspire to pursue when developing smart automation platforms, products and services.

Big Butler technologies often take on the form of digital assistants and bots, for example, which can perform useful tasks for their human users. Big Butler applications increase their users' productivity, accelerate task completion, and can even improve the quality of their work. Big Butler technologies can help a busy white-collar worker reply to e-mails, manage appointments, transcribe voice mails, generate reports, research a topic, book flights, analyse data, schedule vehicle maintenance, all on command and with minimal work. Likewise, Big Butler technologies can help a blue-collar worker create, synch and manage complex plant and/ or fleet schedules; visualize multilayered systems and logistics in real time; automate mobile alerts for certain types of maintenance or production problems; suggest and deliver training for new employees based on their needs, etc. Outside of work, Big Butler applications can help users plan and manage their day, order food, make phone calls, set appointments, adjust a home thermostat, play music, search for movies, manage a home security system, and so on. Just about everything that a butler or personal assistant can do, Big Butler technologies should be able to do as well, and without fear of privacy breaches.

Conversely, Big Mother applications' aim is to take care of you without necessarily asking for your permission. An application that shares your environmental preferences with a hotel ahead of your arrival, for instance, to make sure that the temperature is to your liking, would be an example of a Big Mother technology use. A search engine or browser optimizing its results and ads based on its understanding of your preferences is another. A third might be a universal customized retail experience that follows you around from store to store. While useful, these types of benevolent human–machine partnerships can be a bit overbearing, intrusive and creepy, all while being extremely helpful.

Big Brother applications, however, are all of the technologies that collect data on you, analyse your behaviours, track your movements, follow you online, automatically identify you whenever you pass in front of a CCTV camera or wi-fi beacon, or read your private messages. While sometimes skinned as Big Mother technology use cases (the argument being that data collection and analysis are necessary to create Big Mother services), Big Brother technology applications are by their very nature deceitful, exploitative and hostile. They are the precise opposite of Big Butler technology applications.

Because Big Butler technologies are the types of technologies that most human–machine partnerships should be based on, the ability to easily differentiate between Big Brother, Big Mother and Big Butler technologies is critical. This simple framework should allow industries, governments and consumers to collectively engineer a future in which human–machine partnerships are deliberately steered towards empowerment and human augmentation, rather than towards the systematic erosion of privacy, agency and freedom.

How human–machine partnerships create disruption

Human civilization's most disruptive shifts have been triggered by need. Consider how even the most rudimentary machines, from the bow to the plough, have contributed to economic, social and political disruption. Chronic flooding both motivated and inspired humans to build dykes and artificial water channels. Plagues motivated and inspired humans to discover treatments and cures for their ailments, and to ultimately develop vaccines and medicines which we now all depend on. Every step of the way, from the first tool to the most sophisticated AI, humans have always built machines to help them achieve their goals. Our species is wired to identify problems and pain points, then devise some kind of solution to overcome them. When humanity's principal pain point was hunger, we invented ways of growing and controlling our food supply. When humanity's pain points were thirst and drought, we invented ways of digging deeper wells and irrigating crops more efficiently. When humanity's most pressing pain point was security, we invented walls, weapons and defence strategies to keep threats at bay. This is what our species does: we solve problems. Once we solved the problems that troubled us yesterday, we set out to solve the problems that trouble us today, knowing that once we have solved them, plenty more problems will remain for us to solve tomorrow. With every generation, our tools get better, our machines become more efficient, and our systems become smarter and more autonomous, because that is how we help our tools solve their own sets of problems too.

It doesn't stop there, however. The principal insight we are driving towards isn't that human ingenuity knows no bounds, or that humans have a long history of creating machines to solve problems, improve outcomes and find ways of doing things more efficiently. These things go without saying. The real insight is that humans have always used machines to *enhance* ourselves in some way. Not simply to solve problems, but effectively to become more than what we were without, or before, the invention of the machine we created a partnership with.

What is a farmer equipped with a tractor capable of seeding a hundred acres of fields in the time it would have taken her grandfather to seed a quarter acre, if not a machine-augmented farmer? What is a soldier equipped with automatic weapons, encrypted communications equipment and real-time aerial reconnaissance of the battlefield, if not a machine-augmented soldier? Today, what is a surgeon capable of performing remote surgeries with the help of an Internet connection, specially-designed cameras and finely-tuned robotic arms, if not a machine-enhanced surgeon? The core principle of all human–machine partnerships has been hiding in plain sight all along: beneath all the layers of 'efficiency' and 'velocity' and 'scale', and whatever other practical and measurable benefits we typically assign to human–machine partnerships, lies one simple truth: human–machine partnerships exist, first and foremost, to enhance otherwise limited human abilities.

Becoming aware of this is as important as understanding the difference between Big Brother, Big Mother and Big Butler technology applications, because it informs the most fundamental nature of all human–machine partnerships. It is in this insight that

Human–machine partnerships exist to enhance otherwise limited human abilities.

we find the kernel of the answer to one of the most pressing and contentious questions in our age: will machines replace us?

Or, in the interest of being honest, *will a machine replace me?*

The answer lies at least in part in whether machines have ever been meant to replace us outright, or if they were mostly meant to enhance us. In fairness, the answer has always been both, but when we look at technology disruption throughout history, what we discover is that while some types of machines have, at times, replaced humans outright, most of history has shown that machines have predominantly enhanced us, and liberated us to do more with our most precious resource: time.

What will the future look like?

We don't have to look to a distant horizon or do a whole lot of guessing to begin to answer that question. Physicians have already begun to partner with AIs to improve the accuracy of their diagnoses and reduce unwanted treatment outcomes. Busy executives already leverage digital assistants and specialized bots to automate time-consuming administrative tasks. High-level decision-makers already employ smart analytics products to organize and contextualize data, then transform them into insights. Predictive modelling tools help organizations plan projects and minimize investment risks.

The power of these sophisticated new tools doesn't lie in replacing humans, but in helping them save time, make fewer mistakes, become more effective at their jobs – in short, in *enhancing* them. The world is still a world of humans, for humans, and we should only ever replace humans with machines, not whenever we can, but rather only when we must.

Let's play devil's advocate for a moment and ask why. Why shouldn't we replace humans with machines whenever possible? If a machine is better, faster, more reliable when it comes to delivering accurate diagnoses than a human doctor, why not replace human doctors with artificial ones? And if artificial executives are capable of analysing more data than their human counterparts, and at a higher speed, and also deliver better outcomes for their organization and investors, then why not replace human executives with artificial ones? Why would we not replace humans with machines when machines can be shown to outperform humans?

The short version of the answer is this: when the only objective is increased operational efficiency, machines can indeed often be more efficient than humans, especially when the tasks to be performed are repetitive and predictable. But most tasks – or rather most jobs – are not all that repetitive or predictable. Whether a job has social and collaborative elements, or creative problem-solving elements, or demands human qualities like leadership, inspiration, instincts and improvisation, machines can assist humans but not replace them. Additionally, progress isn't solely a game of improved operational efficiency. Not by a long shot. Progress is also – and perhaps mostly – a game of imagination, innovation, disruption and creative adaptation, at none of which machines, no matter how sophisticated, are better than humans.

Even sophisticated AIs, which can help humans drive towards revolutionary breakthroughs in medicine, material science, microchip design, energy research and a thousand more disciplines, cannot, on their own, do the sort of work that their human partners rely on them to help them with. There is no artificial Steve Jobs, Elon Musk, Jeff Bezos, Satya Nadella or Sundar Pinchai. There is no artificial Stephen Hawking, Steven Weinberg, Peter Higgs or Freeman Dyson. And for that matter, there is also no artificial Margaret Atwood, Doris Lessing, Toni Morrison or Virginia Woolf. In other words, there is no artificial genius, no artificial visionary, no artificial serial innovator, and no artificial leader, and there may not be any of those for quite some time, if ever.

That is the crux of the problem with machines, no matter how sophisticated they become, and how close they can ultimately mimic human thought. What changes the world, the forces that propel the world and humanity forward, are genius, vision,

innovation and leadership, not improvements in repetitive task efficiency, faster computing power or real-time language processing.
Moreover, machines are designed to naturally complement human
limitations, just as we are naturally equipped to complement theirs:
we are, humans and machines, entwined in a symbiotic dance as
old as civilization itself. The equation that has driven disruption
and progress throughout human history has never been *man vs
machine* but rather *man + machine*. That enduring partnership has
turned the wheel of progress throughout human history, and that is
why we should continue to pursue the tried-and-true model of
human–machine partnerships that has put humans on the moon,
mapped the human genome and put all of humanity's knowledge in
the palm of our hand.

How machines can help us become better at adapting to change

If disruption is change, and change is inevitable, then disruption
is inevitable. No matter what the industry, no matter what the
function, change will happen. Maybe not today, maybe not
tomorrow, but disruption is coming.

We have already begun to discuss how machines can help
drive disruption (a topic we will dig deeper into still), but it is
just as important to acknowledge that machines can also help us
adapt to disruption.

For instance, how does a mid-level project manager at a Fortune
500 company protect herself from being replaced by a project
management AI that her company's biggest software vendor keeps
pitching to senior executives? One option might be to work longer
hours, take on more projects, get more face time with the boss,
and develop a reputation for an ambitious hard-worker that gets
things done. A second option might be to start employing the
same type of smart automation product that threatens to replace
her in 6–18 months, but make it assist her, on her terms, thereby

increasing her output, shortening product schedules and significantly improving her project team's outcomes.

At best, the first option will get our industrious project manager noticed and moved to another function when her job is taken over by smart automation. At worst, while her superiors may acknowledge her sudden and conspicuous zeal, sooner or later the outcome of her desperate effort will be burn-out, which will only accelerate her demise.

The second option, however, allows her to get ahead of the impending disruption that would otherwise cost her her job, and perhaps even turn the tables on the company's understanding of how smart automation products should be used. By *adopting* the disruptive technology that would have otherwise displaced her, instead of competing against it, she became its beneficiary rather than its victim. The new model she is developing for herself in plain sight of her superiors is a proof of concept (and a proof of value) for a *human + machine* partnership equation that serves as the antidote to an alternative *human vs machine* equation – a vs equation that would have not only cost her her job but probably delivered less than optimal results for the company.

In a worst case scenario, in which the company manages to somehow learn nothing from her initiative and still replaces her with an automated project management solution, she can now enter the job market with sophisticated smart productivity and human–machine partnership skills that she can apply to her next job. Ideally though, the company she works for realizes

Workers proactively adopting a human–machine partnership mindset can help turn a threat into an opportunity.

that the ideal model is to *enhance* competent, experienced workers with smart automation solutions, not *replace* them, and management pursues an employee augmentation strategy rather than an employee replacement strategy.

This is just one example of how workers proactively adopting a human–machine partnership mindset can help turn a threat into an opportunity: by becoming an early adopter of disruptive technologies, and incorporating these technologies into their daily tasks, at-risk workers may not only be able to protect themselves from the threat of losing their jobs to machines, but see their own careers advanced by new technologies.

The value of human–machine partnerships in a nutshell

Human–machine partnerships are fundamentally equal-opportunity opportunities: anything can potentially be improved in some way by having humans and machines partner to perform a task or pursue an outcome, from making coffee and commuting to work in the morning to helping farmers tend their crops and assisting world leaders in making sound policy decisions. At its core, the value of every human–machine partnership can be defined – and even measured – by the improved outcome it delivers. Whether a human–machine partnership results in discovering a cure for cancer or merely helps a busy working person carve out one hour of quiet relaxation in their otherwise taxing day, the value of that relationship is self-evident in the benefit it creates.

For those who might be curious about measuring the return on investment (ROI) of human–machine partnerships, every such partnership will have to be calculated individually, as all other ROI calculations are performed: essentially by weighing cost against gain. Beyond ROI, gauging the value of human–machine partnerships is both more abstract and more instinctive, but also less daunting. Most of us already do this without realizing it: whenever we start assigning daily tasks to a digital assistant, or learn to use voice-activated interfaces instead of keyboards to save time, or invest in a lawn-cutting robot, or avoid a traffic accident because our car's driver-assist features helped us stay on the road, we naturally gain an appreciation for the value that each new partnership with a machine creates for us. The first step in that process is obviously to seek those opportunities, and embrace human–machine partnerships that can potentially improve some aspect of our lives, at home, at work and all points in between.

CHAPTER THREE

Framing expectations for the next age of human–machine partnerships

What's next for human–machine partnerships?

The next 10 years. Before we dive into all the ways that educators, students, workers, businesses and consumers should prepare for the next age of human–machine partnerships, it may be useful to get a better sense for what to expect from it. Bear in mind that while it can be difficult to see far into the future, let alone with any kind of accuracy, we *can* make reliably educated guesses as to the progress that human–machine partnerships are likely to make in the next 5 to 10 years.

Technology disruption is generally a game of decades. Consider the rolling cycle of transition from cassette tapes to CDs to MP3 players to smartphones to streaming services. Likewise, think about the evolution of the bag phone into the flip phone, then the keyboard phone, then the touchscreen-equipped smartphone, and most recently the voice-interface-equipped smartphone: there too, every decade brings a radical new wave of change. Each of the last five decades is marked by a wide-ranging daisy chain of examples of one generation of technology replacing (or improving upon) the one before it. From music and media, consumer electronics, automobiles and productivity tools to industrial automation, transformative transitions in major technology categories tend to follow a 10-year cycle.

Technology disruption is generally a game of decades.

Even the development of 3G, 4G, 5G and some day 6G standards seems to follow a similar evolutionary pace.

So what do we expect to see with regard to human–machine partnerships in the coming decade? Below are our top 10 predictions:

1 Uncertainty about the future of human–machine partnerships relative to the impact of new technologies on employment will remain a deservedly contentious question. The key question plaguing investments in and mass adoption of smart automation will still be: 'Will machines make my job obsolete?' We feel that, despite this book (and hopefully others like it) this question will not be categorically answered in the next decade.

2 Because smart automation will allow companies to do more with fewer employees, at least with regard to jobs heavily steered towards automatable tasks, the most vulnerable employment categories will remain most at risk. Most notably, manufacturing, repetitive administrative functions, accounting, customer service and financial services professions will be among the most at risk of being automated. We offer ways to address this problem in later chapters, but we expect a lot of companies to turn to automation as a headcount replacement strategy as opposed to automation as a human augmentation strategy, nonetheless. All we can realistically

hope for is to minimize and balance this trend, not eliminate it altogether.

3   Conversely, human augmentation achieved by way of human–machine partnerships (involving smart task automation and support from AIs) will begin to emerge as legitimate alternatives to job-killing automation. Certain categories of jobs are likely to experience a revival – a new golden age. What types of jobs are we referring to? The easiest way to identify them is to look for functions for which bandwidth is a principal pain point. Any function that routinely evokes a 'there aren't enough hours in the day' or 'I wish I could clone myself' or even 'I wish I could be in more than one place at once' complaint from the person assigned to it is a likely candidate. These are the kinds of jobs most likely to immediately turn the next generation of smart automation tools and AIs into the next generation of human–machine partnerships. We will dig deeper into what they are later in the book, but for now, we can tell you that they range from educators, police officers, maintenance crews and sales managers to medical staff, newsroom editors, project managers, business executives and content creators, to name only a few.

4   As new types of human–machine partnerships emerge, new types of jobs will also naturally emerge. Our rationale is this: every new physical machine that gets manufactured requires dedicated engineers, programmers, maintenance technicians and skilled operators. Likewise, every new virtual machine (whether it qualifies merely as software, or more specifically as a cloud solution, a fog solution, or an edge solution) also requires dedicated developers, programmers and skilled operators. In short, the world is going to need an entirely new breed of workers who

As new types of human–machine partnerships emerge, new types of jobs will also naturally emerge.

can either invent new human–machine partnership-focused products, fine-tune human–machine partnership-focused products, or work in partnership with intelligent automation products. While some of these jobs may resemble jobs that exist today, and even bear similar nomenclatures, we can predict with a high degree of confidence that they will be very different in their execution, and far more human–machine partnership-focused than they are today. Others may include entirely new types of roles, like AI ethicists and AI bias moderators.

5 As human–machine partnerships insert themselves into our daily lives over the course of the next decade, everyone touched by this shift will become, on a practical level, a technologist. No matter how intuitive and conversational AI interfaces become, a deeper, richer, multilayered world of human–machine partnerships will require us to become far more savvy, fluent and knowledgeable about the technologies that surround us and enable us to carry out a multitude of daily tasks, both at work and away from work. It would be easy to gloss over this cultural shift, but we feel that it is important to highlight it, because it is fundamental to the growing relationship between humans and machines. As we adapt to becoming increasingly dependent on human–machine partnerships, the fact that we simultaneously teach machines to behave more like humans *and* train ourselves to better care for and teach machines to help manage our daily lives, is incredibly significant.

6 Voice will replace keyboards and typing as the next interface between human and machine. Gestures, eye-tracking and other types of interfaces notwithstanding, voice and natural language will be the next keyboard.

7 Smart automation, machine learning, deep learning and AI will insinuate themselves into not only business functions like time management, task management, communications, collaboration, research, data processing, productivity, quality control, analysis, predictive modelling and decision-making, but also into non-work activities like shopping, commuting,

media consumption, banking, cooking, home life, healthcare, fitness and leisure. As we expect most of these technologies to feel organic, natural and adaptive to their users, these types of technology applications will help steer technology users towards Big Butler-type products and services.

8 Artificial intelligence will drive the next generation of IoT products and solutions. From smart cameras and smart microphones to smart buildings and smart energy grids, the next decade will see most 'dumb objects' become smart, then smarter still. We can already see how driver-assist technologies are paving the way towards fully autonomous vehicles. Similarly, today's smart home products are paving the way towards fully autonomous, self-managing homes. Every connected object that can be made smart can and will be made smarter, more autonomous and capable of having more human-like interactions with users.

9 The combination of smart objects, ubiquitous AI and voice as the new interface will begin making traditionally analogue interfaces like knobs, levers and buttons obsolete. The next decade may see the beginning of an end to 20th-century tropes like mechanical light switches, house keys, television remote-controls, and computer keyboards, and the rise of an entirely new generation of frictionless, voice and gesture-controlled interfaces for home appliances, from stoves and refrigerators to washing machines and lawn-mowers. This signals the beginning of an impending inflection point not only in terms of technology innovation but for our culture as a whole. It is no small detail that evolved primates who have succeeded in evolving into what we are today thanks in great part to our opposable thumbs and tactile dexterity, will now, after millions of years of evolution, begin to interact with our environment with our voice perhaps as much as with our hands. This inflection point is profound and deserves its own conversation.

10 Data security and privacy will continue to present tremendous challenges in an increasingly digital world, but we believe we will get clarity. This is for three reasons: a proliferation of IP-connected cameras, microphones, sensors and devices sitting alongside massive investments in cloud storage and computing services will rightly inflict many a sleepless night on data security and digital privacy experts; in conjunction with this, edge computing and AI will become significantly smarter and more powerful, simultaneously creating entirely new sets of solutions as well as threats; blockchain technologies, used in conjunction with ubiquitous deep-learning algorithms and a combination of edge and fog AI, may some day provide far more effective defences against hackers than exist on the market today, but we aren't quite there yet. Because these defences will exist simultaneously in the cloud, within the network, at the network node level, *and* inside devices (at the data collection point), the types of human–machine partnerships that make us most vulnerable to hackers will become infinitely more secure for users than they currently are, but it may take most of the next decade to get there.

Beyond the next 10 years

In the interest of relying on the kinds of verifiable facts, trends and insights that make us effective business technology analysts, we tend to shy away from fanciful prognostications about the future and what is commonly known in conference circles as 'futurism'. (As much as we enjoy science fiction, we prefer science fact.) This means that our predictions about the future of human–machine partnerships beyond the next decade will be both mercifully short and rightfully cautious. Here, then, are several technology and human–machine partnership trends that we feel comfortable will continue to evolve well beyond the next decade:

1 Artificial intelligence is the future of human–machine partnerships, if for no other reason that now that we know how to inject intelligence into machines, we aren't likely to see machines get dumber. They will only become smarter, and both their utility and value will be defined by their intelligence.

2 20th-century educational models will begin to radically change in the coming decades. How we think about education, how we structure it, how we invest in it, and how we deliver it will become increasingly personalized, mobile and technology-driven.

3 As smart automation technologies evolve, and the nature of work evolves with them, 20th-century models of 'job training' will radically change as well.

4 Unemployed workers from disrupted sectors should not expect universal basic income to come to their rescue, especially in large, dynamic economies which traditionally do not value economic safety nets.

5 Despite what you may have heard from scores of attention-seeking futurists, 'the end of work' is a highly unlikely outcome of the AI revolution. Since consumer spending is the lifeblood of most modern capitalist economies, smart automation replacing human workers at scale is ultimately a self-defeating economic model. We will leave it to economists to debate at what unemployment threshold each particular country's economy will begin to experience stagnation and/or a recession, but regardless of where that threshold falls, it makes the end of human employment impossible for most countries, at least in the next 30 to 50 years.

6 While 'the end of work' is unlikely to result from the next several waves of digital disruption, the nature of work will certainly go through a profound transformation over the

course of the next three decades. We are already seeing the beginning of this with flexible work hours, mobility, new collaboration tools, the rise of the independent contractor class, and the erosion of vertical hierarchy models being normalized across industries. This transformation from the traditional model of employee presence, vertical management hierarchies, regimented office life, and on-premise technology solutions to the much more agile and packable 'work from anywhere with anyone' operational model that digitally-savvy organizations favour today, is only the beginning of what is yet to come.

20th-century educational models will begin to radically change in the coming decades.

What does this mean for businesses?

To properly explore what these changes will mean for business, let's look at enterprise-class businesses and small to medium-sized businesses separately.

Enterprise

Since 2015, the term Digital Transformation has grown into a strategic imperative across the enterprise ecosystem. While business management cynics may, on occasion, refer to it as a buzzword, the fact remains that digital transformation is a fairly accurate way of describing the type of adaptation that businesses need to go through to remain competitive today. Organizations that fail to digitally transform run a very real risk of being unable to compete in an increasingly technology-driven business ecosystem. Companies that fail to adapt to change typically fade into obsolescence.

Our own research on the matter showed that from 2015 to 2018 those companies that had either struggled or failed to keep pace with their industry's digital transformation progress were less competitive than their more digitally-evolved counterparts, more likely to have lost employees, and far less confident about their prospects for the future.[1] Conversely, organizations that had managed to either keep pace or outpace their industry with regard to digital transformation reported being more competitive than they had been before their adaptation, more likely to have created more jobs, and far more positive about their prospects for the future.

Companies that fail to adapt to change typically fade into obsolescence.

What we currently refer to as 'digital transformation' is little more than the latest iteration of a cyclical adaptation to new technologies by the business community. What makes it different from previous versions of it is that this round of adaptation involves so many transformative technologies all at once. Businesses aren't being asked to transition from typewriters to personal computers, or from catalogue mailings to online commerce. They are being asked to adapt to over half a dozen entirely new technologies simultaneously, and fundamentally change every aspect of their business, all at the same time. This is unprecedented in human history.

It isn't yet clear whether we will call the next wave of technology adaptation by the business community 'digital transformation' or something else (our money is on something else), but for now, and for the foreseeable future (until the business world has survived this wave of technology disruption and adaptation), we will continue to refer to it as digital transformation.

Why did we feel it important to bring this up? Because the coming AI revolution, which will drive a new era of human–machine partnerships, is digital transformation's next chapter. And as such, only companies that have already successfully adapted to every new category of technology *currently* driving digital transformation around the world will be in a position to leverage the coming wave of AI-centric disruption. Conversely, companies that fail to digitally transform over the next three to five years, or fail to keep up with the pace of digital transformation across their respective industries, will *not* be able to integrate the types of AI-driven technologies (like smart automation, deep learning and complex predictive modelling) that will drive the next era of human–machine partnerships, and this will put them at a profound market disadvantage.

Our recommendations to enterprise-class businesses are:

1 Accelerate your digital transformation initiatives. If you aren't there yet, get there now. Make it a higher priority than it has been until now. The survival of your business depends on it.
2 Start having conversations with all of your department heads about AI, because not only will AI drive the next phase of your company's digital transformation journey, it will also define its future. (We will dig deeper into what those conversations should look like in Chapter 4.)

Small to medium-sized businesses

Everything that affects the large enterprise also applies to small and medium-sized enterprises or businesses (SMEs or SMBs). But for SMBs, the challenge is different. While the enterprise struggles with agility, velocity, internal politics and scale, SMBs tend to struggle with bandwidth and budgets: who has time to drive digital transformation and learn everything there is to learn about new technologies when so much needs to get done and so few people are available to do it in the first place?

This shortage of capacity is often compounded by the fact that most SMBs may not even have a chief digital officer, or a chief technical officer, or anyone tasked with owning the company's technology roadmap, let alone its change management roadmap. We understand why many SMBs have operated this way until now, and sympathize with the operational prioritization of the *now* at the expense of the *next*. Having said that, SMBs have no choice but to get serious about this, and now. There won't be time to 'catch up' later. If you are an SMB and you plan on still being in business in 2028, you must start becoming a 2028 business now.

If it means hiring a chief digital officer, do it. If it means hiring a consultant or specialized contractor to manage your business's digital transformation for the next three years, do that. If it means attending technology conferences to better understand how new digital technologies are remaking the business world for a new technology-driven world, definitely do that. Whatever it takes, you need to start getting there now. And while you're at it, start paying attention to how AI will soon enable your business to compete against Fortune companies. That is where the real payoff will be. (Again, more on this in Chapter 4.) One glimmer of hope for SMBs is that the solution is hiding in plain sight: if capacity is a problem, and smart automation is designed to help companies solve capacity problems, the solution to your capacity problem is to inject smart automation into your business functions as quickly as you can. The faster you begin the process, the sooner your capacity and operational bandwidth challenges will begin to feel less restricting.

What does this mean for workers?

The coming AI revolution, the one that will bring about a new era of human–machine partnerships, will not only transform the way we work but also the way we think about work.

Expect a shift from traditional definitions of 'white-collar' and 'blue-collar' work to a far more hybrid model that will incorporate elements of both. We also anticipate an increased demand for STEM jobs (science, technology, engineering and maths), the inevitable rise of slightly less advanced and less well-paid STEM-Lite jobs, and the advent of a whole new breed of what we affectionately like to call *next-collar* jobs. We will dig deeper into all of this in Chapter 5, but for now, be aware that the traditional job classifications that we all grew up with will begin to change fairly radically towards the end of the next decade.

Secondly, expect a fairly significant impact on the nature of employment. We aren't only talking about the change from the traditional *full-time employee* models (a staple of the 20th century) to 'the gig economy', the rise of which we are witnessing already, but it is certainly one dimension of that change. For instance, it wasn't unusual for Baby Boomers to work for only one or two companies throughout their entire lives. That was it. For Generation X, that number rose to over half a dozen or more. For millennials, that number may yet triple before they retire (assuming that 'retirement' is a concept that will outlive Generation X). For post-millennial generations, the notion of being 'employed' at all may soon become entirely alien, a relic of the past, as obsolete as office cubicles and fax machines. (More on this in Chapter 5.)

As humans learn to enhance their productivity and capabilities through new types of AI-assisted human–machine partnerships, we also expect our definition of 'work' to evolve. For instance, a worker may, by outsourcing most of her 'busy work' to bots and smart task automation solutions, be able to complete tasks which would have taken a full work day back in 2015 in under two hours. What then, might she do with the six hours she has gained?

Will she fill these hours with more work and more than quadruple her output, or go enjoy the rest of her day with her family? Will she spend the next two hours doing the exact same thing for an entirely different company, and then the next two doing the same for yet another, and then a fourth, allowing her to ultimately collect pay cheques from four separate 'full-time' jobs?

Will she spend her free time learning new business skills, creating art, volunteering at a local charity, tutoring low-performing students, writing her generation's great American novel, contributing to medical research, helping solve pressing environmental problems?

Already, we begin to see how the nature of work, when enhanced through advanced new types of human–machine partnerships, may radically evolve into something far more complex, nuanced and filled with possibilities than the basic model of 'full-time', 'part-time' and 'contract' employment that, until now, dominated Western economies.

Thirdly, it is possible that the erosion of traditional employment, combined with the democratization of sophisticated technologies that will give rise to entirely new categories of human–machine partnerships (whose outcomes we just hinted at) may be the catalyst for a golden age of entrepreneurialism, massive free-associating collaboration and endless ripples of accelerated micro-innovation. What do we mean by all of that?

1 Entrepreneurialism: once workers realize that they can build virtual teams using sophisticated AIs, each capable of performing complex and specialized tasks on their own, they may realize that starting their own business makes more sense than working for someone else. Many of them may initially find themselves forced into it by changes in their industry.

2 Free-associating collaboration: with so many entrepreneurs, private contractors and skilled professionals with newly-found free time on their hands (thanks to the efficiency of their personal human–machine partnership ecosystems), *and* the digital connective tissue linking us all together across a multitude of social and digital platforms, the potential for spontaneous organic collaboration on all manners of pet projects, social causes and large collaborative initiatives increases exponentially.

3 Accelerated micro-innovation: with so many people enjoying a lot more bandwidth *and* the enhanced capabilities of sophisticated AI assistants and deep-learning tools, it stands to reason that at least some of their energies will be spent solving problems for themselves and others, and that wave after wave of these problem-solving initiatives will quickly grow into an ocean of personalized, easily-implemented innovation (or 'micro-innovation').

In other words, we see the coming AI revolution as more of a maelstrom of opportunity for today's workers than a threat to their economic security, but as we will see in Chapter 5, we still have a lot of ground to cover before we can turn those possibilities into a scalable reality. One of the biggest challenges we face in the coming decades is how to ensure open and equitable access to training, skills and technology so that every economic layer in society can both *contribute to* and *benefit from* the next wave of human–machine partnerships.

What does this mean for the world's education and training infrastructure?

Chapter 6 is devoted to answering this question in detail, but now may be a good time to start thinking about the role that educational institutions will have to play in helping us successfully transition forward.

It is time to acknowledge that *education* and *training* are two sides of a same coin, and that, as such, they are simultaneously different and inseparable. This means that we can no longer afford to treat education and job training as disjointed functions to be acquired from institutions that operate at a complete disconnect from one another. Education and job training must be brought closer together. While we must take great care not to ever confuse one for the other, as they serve very different (albeit complementary) purposes we must find ways of connecting them better. The current disconnect between education and job training already doesn't serve our workforce well, and certainly isn't designed to prepare anyone for the types of human–machine partnerships they will need to naturally adapt to, nurture and grow.

What this means is that we cannot adapt to a new AI-driven world in which human–machine partnerships will become part of our everyday lives without changing the way we approach education and job training. Both need to be redefined to properly address the demands of the coming age of human–machine partnerships.

What does this mean for consumers?

Consumers are going to have to deal with a lot of disruption in the way they deal with everyday activities, from buying things and paying their bills to how they experience the world and interact with the world around them.

We, as consumers, are about to step into a world increasingly filled with magical objects: self-driving cars, talking computers, intelligent homes, companion drones, autonomous home appliances, pocket healthcare assistants… . it's going to be a fantastical experience, first for people who can afford the latest gadgets and smart tools, and later for everyone else, as the cost of these new technologies makes them more readily affordable. Everything is likely to change over the course of the next two decades, from how we turn on the light in a room to how we buy and prepare food. Even vacuum cleaners and lawn-mowers operate themselves now.

The flip side of that magical world is that it is filled with sensors, cameras, microphones, algorithms, data, profiling and potentially intrusive technologies that can be used against consumers. Yes, your TV could be spying on you. Yes, your phone could be used to track your movements and habits. Yes, even that health management app could be sending private health data to third parties you know nothing about. And so without sounding the alarm, the dual topic of data security and privacy in general isn't something that is going to go away. We have to address it, and we have to *keep* addressing it until we get it right.

We are about to step into a world increasingly filled with magical objects.

Here, we circle back to the importance of understanding the difference between Big Brother, Big Mother and Big Butler: if consumers understand this with any degree of fluency, they will also understand how important it is to demand nothing less than Big Butler solutions from technology companies that want to grow loyal, enduring and happy customer ecosystems and user bases. Settling for Big Mother solutions (or worse, accepting Big Brother solutions) will not deliver the types of opportunities that a Big Butler-driven model of human–machine partnerships stands to deliver.

What does this mean for technology companies?

The topic of Big Butler vs its alternatives is a perfect segue into this aspect of our discussion: how will technology companies need to adapt in order to remain competitive? By leading the way with Big Butler solutions, and the types of products and services that drive towards positive, empowering, valuable human–machine partnerships. Conversely, how can companies get on the wrong side of the future of human–machine partnerships? By developing Big Brother solutions that create human–machine exploitation use case rather than human–machine partnership use cases. Most of the rest of this book will dive deeper into the latter. *The Future of Human–Machine Exploitation* will have to be the title of another book.

Several other challenges come to mind, which we will dive into a little more in later chapters. One focuses on the challenge of designing solutions for an infinite range of use cases. Think of it this way: a tool is a tool. A computer, like a hammer, is a tool. Tools have specific uses. A narrow range of uses, in fact. A hammer is a hammer. A knife is a knife. A car is a car. And while some tools can serve more than one purpose (the more complex the tool, the more versatile it is), the limitations of their designs inform the limitations of their uses. Even a Swiss Army knife, with all its handy little attachments, can only serve so much purpose. But AI, especially combined with the Internet of Things (IoT), is different in the sense that an infinite combination of uses can be created by simply connecting some kind of AI capability (edge-, fog- or cloud-based) to different devices. That is what makes AI different from every other tool ever devised by mankind. The combination of AI and IoT creates an infinite number of possible use cases for human–machine partnerships. Technology companies that understand how to build for that infinite use case model (essentially a platform model) will find itself at a profound advantage against companies that don't design for interoperability and scale.

Two of the other areas we will dive into in the next few chapters touch on the challenge of redefining the value of technology in the age of commoditized AI, and the pros and cons of building companies around specialized products vs platforms. These two topics burn at the core of everything we have discussed here so far, and how they are addressed by tech companies will, one way or another, shape the next several decades of human–machine partnerships.

CHAPTER FOUR

How businesses should prepare for the next age of human–machine partnerships

The 10-year digital transformation roadmap

We have already done a good deal of writing about leveraging Digital Transformation to not only survive but thrive in the digital economy, and how that kind of technology-driven agility can be turned into a futureproofing model.[1,2]

First, it is imperative that every business becomes a technology company. The days of the IT department being its own island or silo inside an organization are over. IT and technology in general needs to be embedded in every department and every business function, from the most insignificant customer touchpoint to the most critical senior leadership decision. This is not merely an operational transition. It is also a mindset. That mindset must be reflected in the company's identity, and articulated through every investment and decision. In other words, it is not enough to move the IT out of its gated silo and embed it in marketing, sales, HR and other departments. The transition has to be deeper than that: restaurants, automakers, hotels, retailers and airlines can no longer afford to think of themselves merely as foodservice, manufacturing, hospitality, retail and air-travel companies. They must think of themselves as technology companies as well.

This is not a matter of choice. It also isn't a fad or just the latest buzz-phrase to be parroted ad nauseam by endless daisy chains of fickle business consultants. It is reality. The world *is* changing. *Business* is changing. Consumer needs and investor expectations are changing. Business models are being shattered and replaced in real time by successive waves of technology platforms. Everything is being redesigned, from logistics and data analysis to retail and healthcare. Companies that fail to understand just how fundamental this shift is, at every level of their operations, will not survive the transition into an AI-driven economy.

Disney is an example of this. Disney has traditionally been a media and entertainment company. Its focus was on creating content and products, attracting customers and designing remarkable experiences. Disney was a traditional brand, and as such it knew to focus primarily on driving loyalty and delivering exceptional experiences. But Disney was also a company that understood numbers and data, and that technology could not only solve problems but create new opportunities. A few years ago, Disney began revamping its data collection and analysis capabilities, investing in sensor technology and real-time behavioural processing at its parks and other properties, and partnering with technology companies to integrate extensive IoT, machine learning, smart automation, robotic process automation and AI into their most critical and high-volume business applications.

Disney can now follow visitors around their properties, track their purchases, incorporate behavioural analysis into their predictive models, personalize interactions between guests and cast members, and turn all of this into magical experiences, which in turn convert to positive word-of-mouth, recommendations, high customer retention, wallet-share, attention-share and multigenerational loyalty. While Disney's magic has always been a combination of company culture, HR discipline, customer-centric practices and an emphasis on delivering exceptional experiences, much of the magic behind Disney experiences today is *also* powered by technology. Cast members knowing your name and guessing what your favourite dessert might be, frictionless check-ins and payments, reactive environments intelligent enough to adjust to your preferences, marketing communications that are neither annoying nor intrusive.[3] Disney does nearly everything better than it used to because it is now a technology company.

Likewise, small businesses – from independent retailers to law firms – have in recent years embraced new and emerging technologies to remain competitive, improve operational efficiency, reduce costs and grow their clientele. Real estate agents have already begun to leverage virtual reality (VR) and 3D videos to create virtual property tours for potential clients who don't have time to schedule physical visits. Repair shops have begun to use automated scheduling tools to manage customer appointments. Law firms are beginning to rely on AI and machine-learning solutions to proofread contracts and transcribe notes and depositions. Retailers are also increasingly using marketing automation to attract customers to their stores, and AI tools to analyse in-store traffic and purchasing patterns, as well as manage their inventory and automate orders with key vendors.

While global brands and enterprise-class companies and small to medium-sized businesses tend to approach digital transformation and technological adaptation differently, it is now clear that technological adaptation is the path of least resistance for businesses looking to not only survive but thrive. Data we collected for the *2018 Digital Transformation Index* revealed that the faster companies were to adapt to new technologies, the sooner technology disruption evolved into opportunity, growth, market leadership, job creation and a positive outlook on the future.[4] Conversely, companies that struggled to adopt and incorporate new technologies into their business models were more likely to struggle, have a negative outlook on the future, and report that technology disruption had cost them jobs. While some companies may be able to argue that resisting digital transformation has not harmed their business or made them less competitive, they are in the minority. For every other business, evolving with the times, and particularly with technology, is an imperative that must permeate every organizational level and every role, from the most senior decision-maker to the most junior employee.

The principal technology categories we are talking about, at least for the next decade, can be distilled down to the following list:

- cloud computing;
- edge computing;
- machine learning;
- cognitive computing and AI;
- smart automation (virtual and physical) and robotic process automation (RPA);
- wireless connectivity (2G, 3G, 4G, 5G, Bluetooth, wi-fi, etc);
- IoT/IIoT (industrial Internet of Things);
- augmented reality (AR)/virtual reality (VR)/mixed reality (MR);
- 3D printing;
- green tech (renewable energy, green buildings, etc).

Many of the specific technology applications you may be wondering about as you read that list (like autonomous vehicles, smart homes, companion robots and self-managing systems) typically combine several of these technology categories: autonomous vehicles, for instance, combine cloud computing, edge computing, machine learning, AI, smart automation, robotic process automation, wireless connectivity, IoT/IIoT, and quite possibly even some kind of mixed reality.

Three steps to transforming your business

Step 1: Identify technology categories

The first step in outlining a 10-year digital transformation road-map that will adequately prepare a business for an AI-driven economy begins by identifying these technology categories, developing a rudimentary understanding of the types of problems they solve, and building internal competencies focused on the types of opportunities they may create for the business.

Step 2: Technology partners and business function

The second step in that process is two-fold. On the one hand, it is imperative to identify and recruit technology partners that will help your business select, prepare for and deploy specific technology solutions. These could be technology vendors themselves, or third-party technology enablers. On the other hand, every business function that will adopt new technology solutions will have to be rethought, redesigned and reorganized to adapt to its new technological capabilities. This part is important. Digital transformation doesn't merely consist of adding a new technology to an existing business model and carrying on as before. The business function itself will likely have to undergo a significant reimagining and reorganization.

Imagine, for instance, a shipping warehouse transitioning from fixed shelves, human stockers, human pickers and human packers to a system of automated mobile shelving, human stockers and human packers. In this model, human pickers (whose job it was to fetch items from shelves and bring them to the packers) have been replaced by ambulatory robot shelves that deliver the items directly to the packers. Imagine the redesign of the warehouse floor necessary to accommodate this new model. Imagine the technology investments required to make it all work (cloud- and edge-computing solutions, in-house software and hardware solutions, wireless connectivity upgrades, enhanced cybersecurity, etc) as well as the new technical know-how, training and new procedures necessary for this new model to work seamlessly.

This example outlines the extent to which the introduction of a single transformative technology solution into a business ecosystem will radically alter that ecosystem. The same is true of the introduction of an AI tool in the recruiting process, the introduction of smart automation and robotic process automation tools in billing, scheduling and marketing processes, the introduction of visualization and data analytics tools in business intelligence and decision-making processes, and so on. Technology used properly is truly transformative, not merely additive. We emphasize this point to highlight just how vital it is for organizations large and small to understand that the technologies discussed throughout this book are not to be treated as business accessories or mere add-ons. They form the technical foundations of a fundamental evolutionary transformation of every single business function they touch. The second step in a 10-year digital transformation roadmap can only succeed when companies understand and embrace this insight. Disney did, and so too a growing number of companies, from BMW and Whole Foods to Burberry and Southwest Airlines. The trick though, the secret to making it work, is to partner with technology providers and enablers in order to execute. Companies in the early stages of this process cannot, no matter how technology-agile they are, do this quickly and at scale without the right partnerships.

Technology used properly is truly transformative, not merely additive.

Step 3: Company evolution

The third step is to build on previous successes, troubleshoot through friction points, and adapt as quickly as possible to both the challenges and the benefits that come from a digital transformation journey. Typically, during this phase of a company's evolution, technologists have begun to move out of IT and embed themselves in every business function. Many of the specialized competencies that were once the domain of external technology partners have been transferred to internal staff, from standard admin roles to complex coding and customization skills. By this point, decision-makers are not merely knowledgeable about the technology categories that their departments use, but fluent in their use. Identifying, deploying and adapting to new technology solutions is now much faster and easier than it used to be. Change management has become part of the operational model. Agility is being baked into the company's operational culture.

One of the most discernible shifts that companies undergo in this phase deals with focus. While the early days of digital transformation tend to target internally-facing goals, companies begin to turn their attention outward. Instead of asking 'how do we improve operational efficiency' and 'how do we reduce IT costs', the question becomes 'how do we attract more customers', 'how do we increase revenue', and 'how do we become more competitive?' This shift always signals a transition among companies engaged in a digital transformation journey.

Applying change management principles to the coming shift

We've discovered that the six most critical differentiators between technologically agile companies and technologically challenged companies are:[5,6]

- the degree to which the leadership is willing to take risks on big technology shifts early;
- the leadership's ability to quickly develop new operational and revenue models around new technologies;

- the speed with which organizations are able to scale the acquisition of new knowledge and skillsets internally;
- their ability to operationalize change (delegate and empower operational staff with minimal bureaucratic interference);
- a willingness to build proactive partnerships with technology vendors;
- a sense that if they don't get there first, the opportunity will pass them by.

How can this be translated into actionable outcomes? Companies that fail to adapt to change quickly tend to be risk-averse, unclear as to how to convert new technologies into opportunity (most, in fact, tend to regard new technologies more as threats than opportunities), an inability (or unwillingness) to train and empower operational staff, an absence of critical technology partnerships, and no sense of urgency. Conversely, technologically agile, highly adaptable organizations operate more in challenger mode: open to new ideas, open to failing cheaply and fast in order to test and learn an idea's real-world potential, quick to operationalize and monetize, and hungry for any edge they can get over incumbent competitors.

Perhaps the most important trait of agile companies is their proactiveness. They don't wait for things to change or become mainstream. They seek out emerging shifts and work to uncover, test and master them before the rest of their industry. The coming smart automation shift is no different. Companies that want to make the most out of it, be least disrupted by it, and turn it into their biggest strategic advantage over their competition in the next decade need to embrace it hard, fast and early. *Wait and see* is not a sound business strategy in the age of technology disruption and smart automation for the same reason

Wait and see is not a sound business strategy in the age of technology disruption.

that *also in* is never a sound brand differentiation strategy. For businesses to reap the benefits of the coming age of human–machine partnerships, they must adopt the change management principles listed above: courage, clarity of vision, operational agility and velocity.

Translated into practical operational advice:

- take risks on big technology shifts early (in this case, smart automation and robotic process automation);
- quickly develop and test new (or improved) *organizational* and *operational* models;
- quickly develop and test new *revenue* models;
- scale and accelerate the acquisition of new knowledge and skillsets internally;
- empower operational staff while minimizing bureaucratic interference and roadblocks;
- build proactive operational partnerships with technology vendors;
- whatever your adaptation timelines are today, cut them in half.

Finding the right balance between automation and augmentation

The first rule of not investing in the wrong technologies (or not applying them to the wrong problems) is: don't fall for the siren song of automation as the solution to everything. Not everything can be automated, not everything should be automated, and not everything that can be automated should be. Leading a modernization effort with 'how can we make this technology fit into our business' is the wrong approach. The correct approach is to ask what problems it can solve, whether those problems are worthy of solving at the overall cost of that new technology, and what kinds of risks and opportunities that technology can also open up.

This will be different for every industry or organization. A restaurant chain has different automation and augmentation needs from a hospital. Even within a complex organization, IT, marketing, production, billing, shipping, distribution, HR and engineering will have wildly differing automation and augmentation needs. For that reason, there is no simple equation businesses can apply to this question, no golden ratio, no 80/20 rule. Every single case is unique.

Don't fall for the siren song of automation as the solution to everything.

Some automation decisions are simpler than others. If a robot or automated system can produce more widgets per day than human workers, do it as well or better than human workers, do it with equal or better consistency than human workers, and/or do it more cost-effectively than human workers, then it makes sense to replace human workers with robots and automated systems. Some tasks are purely about efficiency. Human traits like creativity, insight, collaboration, abstract thinking, problem-solving, and troubleshooting, are irrelevant to their success. If anything, those traits might actually interfere with them. Even when automation of this type kills jobs, it makes little business sense to resist automating them. If a business cannot be as or more efficient than its competitors, it cannot remain competitive, and if it cannot remain competitive, the few jobs it failed to replace with automation will end up costing it a lot more jobs when its weakened value to the market causes it to start failing. For that reason, any job that doesn't require creative, collaborative, insightful input or flair from a human worker should be automated if it can be. For every other kind of job, however, augmentation through selective automation may be a better bet.

The trick is to differentiate between jobs and tasks. When you take a step back and look at what any job consists of, you will find that it consists of a series of tasks. Certain tasks can be automated. Other tasks cannot. The more tasks a job consists of that can be automated, the more that job is likely to find itself at risk. The fewer tasks a job consists of that can be automated, the more likely a human worker in that job is to be augmented by selective automation. Example: an assembly line worker's only task, all shift long, may be to line up two parts delivered by parallel conveyor belts, and push a button. In another part of the building, however, an engineer's daily tasks may include designing new parts, verifying tolerances and dimensions on quality control samples, attending product development meetings, signing off on new assembly drawings, interviewing new hires, mentoring junior-level engineers in her department, meeting with technology vendors, walking the production floor, attending a product or machine demo, tracking the progress of dozens of ongoing projects, drafting monthly reports, entering new parts into the company's inventory system, reviewing budget proposals, and on, and on, and on. Some jobs consist of only a handful of tasks. Other jobs consist of dozens, sometimes hundreds of complex and multilayered tasks. If tasks, not jobs, are what ultimately get automated, the more a job resembles a task (or a small number of repetitive tasks), the more easily it can be automated. The more a job consists of dozens upon dozens of complicated tasks that require a complex multilayered web of skillsets, on the other hand, the *less* likely it is that it can be automated.

'Job automation' is the wrong terminology, and the wrong way to think about the problem of automation killing jobs. When we talk about automation, no matter how rudimentary or sophisticated, we are always talking about *task automation*, not job automation. Always.

Caution: imposing automation where none is needed, or imposing an automation solution that is ill-designed to serve the needs of a particular job function on a human worker, can cause more harm than not automating an automatable task at all. Many of us have worked for companies whose task automation solutions and internal systems, instead of making our lives easier, ended up causing more headaches than they solved, and more work than they saved.

A collaborative, inclusive and empowered workforce decision-making model is essential to the success of effective human worker augmentation endeavours. We see this user-driven technology adoption model already manifesting itself in BYOD (bring your own device) and parallel BYOA (bring your own app) policies increasingly enacted by adaptable, millennial-friendly organizations as a means to reduce operational friction, and empower workers to create their own collaboration and task automation ecosystems. Popular collaboration apps like Slack and Cisco's Webex Teams, seizing on this trend, already offer scores of virtual bots to their users to help them build their own task automation workflows. The lesson here may be that when left to their own devices, digitally agile workers will find ways to augment themselves through smart automation without being asked to. Organizations that learn to spot this behaviour can adapt it in two ways: first, by hiring and developing digitally agile workers; and secondly, by rethinking their approach to IT.

IT and HR: a new chapter in internal collaboration

There are essentially two operational models for IT today: centralized and decentralized. Centralized IT operates much like a command-and-control silo for all technology solutions inside the organization. Decentralized IT has a flatter, more mesh-like structure that allows it to embed itself into the organization's business functions and partner more granularly with operational staff. A decentralized IT model doesn't necessarily mean that the organization's technology enablement teams don't answer to a hierarchy of IT managers all leading back to a chief technology officer (CTO). It just means that IT staff embedded in various business units or tasked with enabling technology solutions on the fly have the independence and autonomy to deliver precisely the types of technology solutions that their users need, and in the format that they need them.

The ability enjoyed by digitally agile companies to quickly test and adapt new technology solutions, accelerate the acquisition of new knowledge and internal skillsets, empower operational staff, minimize bureaucratic interference and roadblocks, and scale technology adoption across the organization can be traced back to a decentralized approach to IT. By decentralizing IT, and embedding IT professionals across the organization, individual IT specialists can become technology enablement agents for each and every job function they collaborate with. This means that, instead of IT being removed from the day-to-day needs and pains of operational staff, they are working right alongside them in the trenches, where they can clearly see what technology solutions will be most helpful, effective and deployable.

What this suggests is that decentralized IT should proactively seek to find new ways to augment human workers and human teams with smart automation and robotic process automation solutions. In other words, they should not wait to be asked to solve a problem, but should *recommend* new opportunities for greater operational efficiency and improved outcomes to the teams they work with. This shift in the relationship between IT and the teams served by IT would be reflected by IT's new role, not only as technology *enabler* but as technology *advisor*.

Here is where this type of thinking deviates from the norm. According to Fuze's 2017 *How CIOs are Shaping the Future of Work* report, most IT departments are still regarded by most organizations as cost centres.[7] This manifests itself in leadership teams in the most common objective handed down to IT departments year after year: cutting costs. Although technology drives business more than ever, and technology investments ultimately drive the majority of improvements in operational efficiency through smart automation, most business

IT must be recognized as the core driver of business.

leaders fail to treat IT departments as the goldmines of opportunity they are. And because of this, they fail to invest in their budgets with an appropriate degree of initiative. The result is that IT departments, instead of being asked to proactively help guide the business development and strategic vision of the companies they serve, end up being relegated to reactive, technical service-type functions. This IT-as-a-cost-centre world view is incompatible with business success in the age of technology disruption.

The solution: IT must be recognized as the core driver of business growth that it has become, and the CTO's insights into how the organization should plan for the future must be placed on equal standing with the COO's. The role of IT must evolve to that of an embedded specialty attached to each business function whose job is to advise, enable and guide human workers and human teams in their evolution towards the best possible mix of automation and augmentation.

What does HR have to do with any of this? First, a company that wants to be agile needs to rethink the way it hires and trains its staff: the days of hiring talent based mostly on their experience and professional skillset are over. HR departments that fail to recognize the importance of human traits like resilience, adaptability, creativity and initiative in their candidate selection process will not be staffing their organization with the types of agile, motivated, innovative problem-solvers that technologically-capable companies will need to adapt to successive waves of technology disruption. An organization cannot operationalize agility and rapid adaptation if it fails to hire agile and adaptive people. It's as simple as that.

Secondly, in fast-changing markets in which scaling skills acquisition and training is paramount to an organization's ability to adapt quickly to disruption, HR departments must become more proactive in developing internal training and upskilling programmes. They must also be more diligent in their analysis of who across the organizations they serve need what training and when. Identifying individual workers' skills and knowledge gaps with some precision is as vital to the success of that organization as delivering the training itself.

Here is where artificial intelligence, deep learning and smart automation may find one of their most useful uses in business organizations of all sizes: by analysing human workers' skillsets, identifying who may need what training, creating (or selecting) training programmes to fill those needs, and delivering them to each individual worker, skills gaps that threaten to slow down an organization's ability to adapt quickly to change and operationalize new business imperatives can be ironed out with little to no need for human intervention.

Organizations have already begun to test gamification schemes in support of this process, to improve worker engagement, awareness of workplace resources at their disposal, and to *incentivize* them to increase their participation in training and upskilling programmes.[8,9] This model is still nascent and has not yet received the positive attention it deserves, but companies that invest in it and rethink their approach to employee development, much in the same vein as they should rethink how to prioritize the traits and soft skills of job applicants they ultimately hire, will find themselves at an advantage over companies that fail to bake agility and continuous skill-building into their operational DNA.

What types of human–machine partnerships should businesses prioritize?

Every business and every human worker have their own unique sets of operational challenges to overcome, so outlining every possible use case of human–machine partnership across every industry and role isn't really practical at this juncture. In order to answer the question, we must look at specific industries, individual businesses and each human worker in detail, identify the challenges and opportunities that human–machine partnerships might be helpful with, and prioritize them. Even then, prioritization can be difficult as challenges and opportunities that may be most important to them may not be addressed by way of smart automation just yet. In other words, what *can* realistically be done now may have to be prioritized over what isn't quite possible just yet. Below is a short list of examples of human–machine partnerships that organizations large and small, for-profit and not, should use as a starting point when thinking about how to augment their human workers in the coming decade.

Accounting and financial planning

Smart search algorithms can increase the number of accounts, filings and records that a single accountant can manage by being able to sift through millions of pages of documents and spreadsheets to flag errors that would have otherwise taken thousands of hours to check. An accountant, thus augmented by this capability, would be free to focus on correcting the errors rather than looking for them, which is a much more productive use of a skilled professional's time.

An AI can also make recommendations as to how to correct each error, or alternatively, an AI can propose several alternative solutions in order to help quickly select the best possible option.

A recommendation engine can propose alternative filings or accounting mechanisms to make better use of certain accounts that may have been underutilized or overlooked. Similarly, an AI can identify areas of financial inefficiency, flagging underperforming accounts or business units, and recommending corrective courses of actions and various remedies.

As with most human–machine partnerships, a professional, experienced human is responsible for making sure that the smart automation tools are performing as needed, makes all of the high-level decisions associated with the accounts, and is ultimately responsible for making the judgement calls upon which those decisions are predicated. This balance between human and machine is what organizations should strive towards.

Agriculture and farming

A combination of IoT, machine learning, machine intelligence and smart automation can help farmers monitor rainfall, the moisture content of fields, soil quality, surface temperature, wind speeds, surface evaporation rates and changes in weather. It can also help alert farmers to the presence of environmental pollutants and pests; possible vandalism of equipment and resources; the possible theft of equipment, livestock, or grain; crop tampering and damaging weather events. These technologies can help give farmers real-time information on every square inch of their farming operation and help them optimize their investments, activities and resource usage to achieve the best possible outcome while minimizing waste.

Smart automation and robotic process automation also promise to bring self-driving autonomy to farming equipment and IoT and data analytics can also help ranchers track and manage their livestock, monitor their health, optimize their growth and plan for their sale.

Drones and other autonomous robots may also provide additional year-round capabilities for farmers lacking the manpower to monitor large acreages, perform heavy-duty manual work, transport heavy loads or perform repetitive precision tasks.

Business management AIs can also help farmers manage their finances; alert them to areas of potential financial, legal and regulatory exposure; recommend corrective action where it is needed; highlight opportunities they may not have considered; monitor global commodities markets and shifts in trade policies for opportunities and threats; monitor equipment and land sales they might be interested in taking a closer look at; and recommend best practices and new technologies they may not have yet considered.

Business management

AIs can assist decision-makers with both prompted and proactive searches, to quickly equip them with the data, information and insights they need, thereby reducing the amount of time they might waste searching for it themselves or waiting for a human assistant to find it and communicate it.

AIs can be programmed automatically to collect, combine, organize and analyse data sets, and convert them into interactive dashboard visualizations that provide managers and decision-makers with the information they need in a digestible, usable format.

Predictive analysis engines can create forward-looking models based on existing data and pattern analysis algorithms to help decision-makers test and understand the potential impact of decisions on future performance. These decisions can range from technology investments and product release schedules to advertising buys and mergers and acquisitions.

Recommendation engines can help business leaders and managers streamline their decision-making process, accelerate their path to a solution, and improve outcomes. Business analytics AIs can also be tasked with identifying hidden business opportunities based on industry, economic and socio-cultural trends.

Robotic process automation software can also continuously collect data from multiple project teams and business units to give business managers real-time visibility to every aspect of the business for which they are responsible. These dashboards can focus on a nearly endless mix of items, from project timelines and budget spending to maintenance schedules and incident reports. Every manager in an organization can leverage robotic process automation to create dashboards about anything they need, from sales to production, shipping, inventory and equipment outages.

Smart automation can also gauge business or employee performance and flag high performers, low performers, and (based on trending) elements at risk of becoming low performers. Recommendation engines can also assist managers in identifying corrective actions and remedies.

In a strange twist of irony, robotic process automation can also pick up the slack for ineffective and underperforming managers. For instance, RPA can be used to automate schedules for hourly workers days, sometimes weeks in advance (as opposed to finalizing schedules at the last possible minute), allowing employees more time to plan for childcare, school, family time, and balance other professional obligations.[10] By making an operational improvement as simple as publishing schedules sufficiently in advance to allow employees to feel less stressed about it, business is likely to improve employee turnover, morale and engagement. Food for thought when brainstorming AI and RPA uses for your business: finding ways to improve poorly managed business processes and outcomes through automation in spite of poor management, and in many cases *because* of it, is not a bad place to start.

City management and planning

AI solutions, coupled with 3D virtualization engines, can help city planners and city managers accurately project current and future strains on utilities and infrastructure, enabling them to identify, budget for and schedule critical improvements accordingly.

AI solutions and 3D virtualization engines can assist transportation investments and upgrades, commercial construction projects, public space expansions, zoning, public safety, utilities improvements, and pedestrian access to minimize traffic congestion; and can improve public services, increase the footprint of green spaces and public parks, reduce environmental pollution, improve the city's overall energy efficiency, reduce crime, provide better access to emergency services, improve the performance of wireless connectivity services, provide robust high-speed broadband Internet capacity in high-traffic areas, and generally help plan for improvements that will prepare today's cities for the capabilities they need to invest in for the future.

Analytics tools and predictive modelling algorithms can also help city managers test various tax collection schemes, the potential impact on X of changes to local ordinances and laws, and the potential cost of failing to invest in certain critical technologies and infrastructure improvements.

Smart automation and robotic process automation can help human city services managers supervise rather than manually control complex essential systems, from traffic lights and parking meter maintenance to litter control and emergency response.

Lastly, robots can assist human workers in a variety of tasks, ranging from litter collection and green spaces maintenance to public transportation, roadways safety and crime prevention.

Construction

Mechanical exoskeletons and power suits or specialized robots can augment the capabilities of human workers in those construction jobs that require the lifting, hauling and guiding of heavy loads, and in some instances high-precision work like cutting and assembly. Robot bricklayers can help human masons lay bricks with laser-like precision. Robot carpenters can make a precise cut in seconds, get it right the first time, and with no risk of injury to the human workers they are tasked with assisting. Robot plumbers could some day install perfect joints in PVC pipe and pressure-test systems in a fraction of the time it takes a team of human plumbers to do the same work, and with fewer errors. Again, the objective of injecting specialized robots into the mix isn't to replace human workers but rather to assist them, make them more efficient, and free them to focus on more high-value tasks.

Using a specialized robot cuts down the amount of time it takes a human to do the same amount of work, allowing professional labourers to finish a job faster. For large projects, this could mean the difference between being able to handle 30 construction projects per year and being able to handle 70 construction projects per year. For smaller jobs, like repair calls, a skilled tradesman augmented by a specialized robot might be able to convert those efficiency gains into a higher number of calls per day. An augmented plumber being able to handle 20 calls per day instead of just 12, for instance, could be a game-changer for that plumber's ability to increase revenue and gain an advantage over his competitors.

AIs can also help humans plan and manage construction projects with minimal input, freeing them to spend more time making calls, closing deals, inspecting work, supervising job sites, schmoozing clients, putting out fires, and focusing on the million little intangible things that only humans can juggle in such a chaotic and fluid environment.

Entertainment

AIs can be taught to write scripts and music. AIs can be taught to create visual effects, enhance images and sound, seamlessly stitch together images and backgrounds, synchronize tracks and media layers, integrate visual effects and objects into scenes, render complex textures, and blur the lines between what is real and what is fake. An entire new ecosystem of visual effects (VFX) artists, coders and digital editors has cropped up in the entertainment industry.

Again, the idea isn't to replace humans with machines, but to augment the capabilities of humans in their respective industries. Thirty years ago, most visual effects in the entertainment world were analogue. Artists painted sets and backgrounds, make-up was applied on actors, prosthetics and mechanical effects were the norm. These labour-intensive methods were expensive to develop and create, slow to set up for shoots, and not particularly convincing. Today, by partnering with sophisticated machines and increasingly intelligent algorithms, technical artists can create three-dimensional photorealistic worlds, creatures, virtual prosthetics and effects, without interfering with principal photography and shoot schedules.

While we expect to see more AI-generated scripts, ads, music, lyrics, videos and other contents, we also expect that these 'creative' AI capabilities will ultimately be used by artists, composers, writers, producers and other entertainment professionals to streamline their creative process, break through writer's block, fine-tune their creations and accelerate production.

Healthcare

AI, deep learning and big data analytics technologies, when applied to genetic data, can help doctors and patients identify vulnerabilities to certain types of medical conditions. By isolating certain key risk factors, and combining them with family history, lifestyle parameters and genetic predispositions, deep learning algorithms can also help draw medical professionals' attention towards areas of potential trouble, thereby informing preventative care.

AI and deep learning algorithms can also assist physicians in delivering more accurate diagnoses in shorter timeframes, and with less probability of errors. AI and deep learning tools can also automatically cross-reference medical records to flag possible drug interaction and sensitivity risks before greenlighting a prescription.

AIs can also be leveraged to manage insurance claims, payment plans, appointments, scheduled check-ups, medical device data collection, medical device data analysis, and scores of other categories of data and records that, together, form the SumTotal of a patient's medical history.

Surgical and medical robots can augment hospitals, outpatient facilities and mobile medical units tasked with performing specialized and automatable precision procedures. These can range from performing heart surgery to 3D printing dental implants. Surgical robots can, in some cases, allow complex surgeries to be performed more quickly and with less scarring, allowing patients to spend less time in recovery and get back to their lives sooner.

3D virtualization, deep learning and AI can also be applied to complex diagnostics, customized care and surgical planning. Scans of blood vessels or organs, for instance, can be made into 3D models and used by surgeons to practise tricky surgeries before performing them on the patient. This new methodology allows for more trial and error before a surgery, increasing its chances of success. This can be especially useful when dealing with aneurysms, bypass surgeries, and the insertion of surgical devices like pacemakers and stents.

Medical researchers are currently teaching AIs to detect every kind of disease imaginable as well as – if not better than – human doctors. Example: Moorfields Eye Hospital in London, in partnership with UCL and Google Deep Mind, have taught an AI to diagnose dozens of individual eye diseases based on 3D scans.[11] This type of AI-assisted human–machine partnership model can be applied to cancer, Alzheimer's, diabetes, mental illness, and pretty much any health challenge that patients and their doctors have worked together for generations to address.[12,13]

Therapy and recovery are also increasingly seeing technologies like VR, sensors, video games, personable AIs, smart toys, wearables and caretaker robots make their way into the fray. These technologies can assist patients and healthcare professionals measure and manage pain, stress, anxiety, depression, loneliness and even shock, thereby accelerating and facilitating patient treatment and recovery. VR technologies are also being used to: help with patient rehabilitation after brain injuries and strokes; help restore patient motor function, posture and balance; and treat post-traumatic stress.[14]

Once again, because it bears repeating, these technologies are not meant to replace healthcare professionals, but rather to augment their capabilities by automating time-consuming processes that have traditionally eaten up valuable time that could be better spent with patients or on research; by accelerating and improving the outcome of diagnoses, treatments and surgeries; by minimizing risk; and by equipping healthcare professionals and patients with powerful new tools that empower them to make better decisions and deliver better medical outcomes.

Two of the most promising niches of technology-augmented healthcare services are eldercare and homecare. Between telemedicine, the IoT, AIs, robotic process automation and intelligent automation, medical professionals and caretakers can remotely monitor the health and well-being of their patients, interact with them through telepresence, automate food deliveries and remotely supervise the administration of medication. Healthcare professionals and caretakers can also assign AIs and caretaker robots to keep their patients company, keep their minds active, track their vitals, automate meal preparation and house cleaning, automate and manage their daily schedules, provide them with a broad range of virtual and analogue treatment and therapy options, and shorten response times in case of an emergency. Not only does this potentially improve patients' quality of life by giving them more autonomy and working towards more favourable healthcare outcomes, it also promises to reduce strain on generally overburdened health systems.

Human resources

HR departments are already able to use AI, machine learning and big data analytics to sift through thousands of resumés in search of the ideal candidate. As we have seen earlier in this chapter, AI bias has highlighted one of the vulnerabilities of relying too much on machine algorithms to make *decisions* for humans. Our view is that humans and machines, working together, plug some of the gaps that humans alone, and machines alone, cannot plug on their own. Algorithms can help flag certain candidates for human recruiters, who can then gauge the quality of the applicants selected for them against a control group of human-selected applicants and desired outcomes, and fine-tune the process until it can be trusted. The candidate selection itself, however, should not be handled by machines but ultimately entrusted to human recruiters. Algorithms should only be used to identify, rate, flag and recommend applicants, not select or hire them.

HR departments can also use AI and deep learning algorithms to help quantify and track employee performance, identify areas of potential improvement, suggest useful training and skill-building resources, schedule and gamify said training, assist managers in motivating, developing and retaining promising employees, help give workers greater visibility to career opportunities, provide employees with the tools they need to better manage their careers, and even alert managers when a valuable employee's behaviour suggests that they may be about to quit. (Yes, AIs can predict that as well.)

Journalism

We have already seen AIs begin to publish their own news report. The *Washington Post*'s 'robot journalist', named *Heliograf*, notoriously published several hundred news stories about the Summer Games in Rio de Janeiro in 2016, and has been publishing stories ever since.[15] *USA Today*, the Associated Press and other news-reporting publications, have turned to AI and robotic process automation for a variety of uses, from compiling research data and fact-checking background information for stories to automating content publishing across dozens of platforms and writing the stories themselves.

At a time when journalism appears to be shrinking, and the consolidation of media companies cuts more journalism jobs than it creates, robot journalists that can write stories normally assigned to human journalists might seem counterproductive and even ominous. The question that naturally comes to mind is: 'Will machines replace journalists too?' But the answer is no. Consider what the business of journalism consists of, besides PR and advertising: substantial journalism work, and the less substantial filler that doesn't require a whole lot of effort or time to put together. The former is high-value work. Some of it might take on the form of months-long investigations and deep investigative journalism. Some of it is less involved but equally important, relevant and difficult to get right. Every day, thousands of passionate, talented, brilliant journalists work themselves to the bone to bring us award-winning reporting on the world's most important stories.

And then you have the other kind of news content: the one-paragraph news updates, the latest sports scores, the closing bell numbers, the police reports, the news bulletins. Those items can be automated. They don't require live journalists to waste their time transcribing information that an AI can reformat and push out on its own millions of times per day. And here is where robotic process automation like this actually helps journalists. By automating the fluff items that can and *should* be automated, news organizations and the journalists they employ are free to focus on stories and assignments that matter. News and stories with more substance. Again, what we see is AI and smart automation being used to allow skilled professionals to focus on high-value work instead of wasting their time on tedious, low-value work.

AI and smart automation can also help alert news organizations to breaking news faster than traditional means, identify trends, better understand their readers' interests, measure the value of various social platforms, test different headlines for the same articles in different markets, fine-tune their wordcount (does an 800-word article consistently perform better than a 900-word article, for example?), customize their readers' newsfeeds, quickly fact-check public statements made by dubiously credible individuals, edit and fine-tune copy, suggest layouts, select images and infographics for use with an article, and so on.

Manufacturing, warehousing and logistics

This is one area in which robotic process automation, the IoT, AIs and autonomous vehicles are most likely to replace human workers at scale. In geofenced ecosystems especially, which represents nearly 100 per cent of manufacturing plants and warehouses, autonomous and semi-autonomous robots will soon be capable of performing most tasks once performed by workers. From fully autonomous mail sorting and distribution facilities to fully autonomous automobile assembly plants, every repetitive geofenced process that can be automated will be. This does not mean that all plants will be able to automate fully, or that most businesses will find value in attempting it, but the next evolutionary wave of manufacturing and warehousing design will lean towards full automation.

The most interesting next wave of innovation for these smart automation environments will not be advancements in computer vision, robot autonomy or computing intelligence (although these categories of innovation certainly are as important as they are fascinating) but rather the consolidation of operating systems.[16] Currently, interoperability between robotic and autonomous systems for use in complex manufacturing and warehousing environments is inefficiently complex. Some kind of standardization with regard to operating systems is overdue, and we expect that the next 5 to 10 years will reveal the winners in that technological arms race.

With regard to human workers in manufacturing and warehousing environments, we still expect engineers and technicians to help install, build, program, maintain, upgrade and repair robots and systems, and perform a wide range of support roles, from providing physical security to supervising robots during non-routine operations, but the age of the fully-automatable warehouse and manufacturing plant is upon us.[17] Perhaps the best way to visualize human–machine partnerships in fully-automated plants where humans and robots do not share the floor in a balanced division of labour is to divide each plant into two floors: a fully-automated floor in which the high-volume work of the plant or warehouse is done by machines, and a floor where human engineers and technicians work in support of the overall operation.

Retail

In addition to aspects of retail already covered in this chapter, robotic process automation can also enable retailers – especially grocery retailers – to automate the picking and packing of products purchased online. The model is simple: a customer submits his shopping list online, and selects a time for delivery or pickup. If he chooses to pick up his items at the store, the contents of his shopping cart will be ready when he pulls up. If he chooses delivery, a vehicle (probably autonomous at some point) will deliver the contents of his shopping cart to his door. Where the robotic process automation comes in is in the sorting and packing. Using warehousing and sorting robots, every item on the shopper's list can be located, picked and added to a physical shopping cart without human intervention. We expect to see grocery retailers testing this fully-automated order fulfilment model, coupled with pickup and delivery options, in the next few years.

133 million new and emerging automation-related jobs could be created between 2019 and 2022.

Hiring and training for a new class of machine-adjacent roles

Businesses should plan to hire and train for entirely new types of machine-adjacent roles and skillsets. Based on the World

Economic Forum's (WEF) projections, 133 million new and emerging automation-related jobs could be created between 2019 and 2022, possibly taking the place of 75 million jobs and roles.[18]

According to the WEF's study, the top 10 declining jobs are:

- data entry clerks;
- accounting, bookkeeping and payroll clerks;
- administrative and executive secretaries;
- assembly and factory workers;
- client information and customer service workers;
- business services and administration managers;
- accountants and auditors;
- materials-recording and stock-keeper clerks;
- general and operations managers;
- postal service clerks.

All of these roles, you will have guessed, are becoming increasingly automatable.

The WEF's study also identifies the following occupations and roles as topping the list of 133 million new and emerging jobs:

- data analysts and scientists;
- AI and machine learning specialists;
- software and applications developers;
- software and applications analysts;
- sales and marketing professionals;
- big data specialists;
- digital transformation specialists;
- new technology specialists;
- organizational development specialists;
- information technology services.

Very few of these roles are automatable, and the vast majority of them, unsurprisingly, involve human–machine partnerships.

How SMBs/SMEs will benefit from more synergy between humans and machines

While it may seem that enterprise-class organizations will benefit from smart customer relationship management (CRM) tools, intuitive enterprise resource planning (ERP) solutions and robotic process automation, the truth is that all smart automation and AI solutions help level the playing field for small and medium-sized businesses. Most of these solutions are available as software-as-a-service (SaaS) offerings that require very little upfront investment and only minimal on-premise IT infrastructure. As these tools become increasingly intelligent and autonomous, particularly with the integration of AI capabilities, which can replace coding and complex technical skillsets with intuitive controls, easily customizable fields and natural language processing algorithms, the barriers of entry – both financial and technical – are disappearing. This means that in terms of computational capabilities, process automation and AI functionality, SMBs are not necessarily at a disadvantage when it comes to accessing and deploying the sorts of digital tools that we've discussed throughout this book. Small and medium-sized businesses can augment their staff and departments with smart automation and AI tools just like large businesses, and benefit from the same operational advantages as their larger competitors.

Smart automation and AI solutions help level the playing field for small and medium-sized businesses.

This insight also applies to one-person businesses or independent contractors. A lone employee can automate billing, smoothly manage collaboration projects with multiple agency teams simultaneously, assign bots to handle routine tasks, use an AI to quickly resolve problems or search for solutions, leverage dashboards to keep an eye on critical metrics, automate reports and filings,

automate scheduling, automate e-mail blasts and routine communications, manage appointments and conference calls.

The benefits are as follows. Traditionally large businesses may
increasingly find that hiring contractors or partnering with
small, specialized firms may be preferable to hiring and training
full-time employees for highly specialized and difficult-to-fill
roles. It also means that small and medium-sized companies may
have the tools to both scale *and* partner together more easily to
compete against larger organizations. Finally, enterprising entrepreneurs may find that by taking control of their own digital
ecosystem, and augmenting themselves with their own process
automation solutions and dedicated teams of specialized AIs and
bots, going solo is more lucrative and preferable to seeking
traditional forms of employment. This may present HR departments and corporate recruiters with a new challenge: in an age
of increased threat of career obsolescence because of automation, candidates with the most relevant qualifications and the
most valuable skillsets may be more difficult to recruit than ever.

CHAPTER FIVE

How workers should prepare for the next age of human–machine partnerships

Futureproofing careers in the age of smart automation

Over the course of the next few decades, machine learning, smart automation and artificial intelligence will transform business operations as radically as the Internet, cloud computing and mobility did. The principal difference between these two waves of technology disruption is their potential impact on job creation. Why? Because while the Internet, cloud computing and mobility served to reinvent the world's IT, logistics and communications infrastructure, machine learning, smart automation and artificial intelligence serve to reinvent the nature of work itself.

Infrastructure plays tend to be expansive, which generally means an increase in labour: people have to learn new skills, new job functions have to be created, and growth drives a need for an increased demand in operational capacity. The most common friction points we observed during the first wave of digital transformation (the one that required that businesses adapt to the Internet, mobile commerce and cloud computing) were generally inadequate budgets, a knowledge and skills gap in the workforce, and an institutional inability to scale quickly. In light of this, it isn't all that surprising that the next wave of technology disruption, which will turn into the next digital transformation for businesses, aims to address these exact pain points: budgets (cost), skills and scale. The problem though is that the core premise of the new generation of technology solutions is that machines can do the work of humans at a lower cost, faster, better, and with virtually no obstacles to scale.

This may help explain why you may have noticed so many economists, business analysts, journalists, lawmakers, educators and workers' rights experts convey their concern for the impact that the three technology categories – machine learning, smart automation and artificial intelligence – may have on the future of employment. Many worry that the more businesses can legitimately automate processes and functions that machines can do at least as well as humans (if not better), the less they will need human workers. This could result in mass layoffs, high unemployment, and ultimately the need to rethink economic models. If the rise of smart automation does indeed lead to an era of permanent unemployment for large swathes of the working age population, how will we, as societies, tackle this problem?

Universal basic income (UBI)

One idea that has attracted supporters is for governments to provide their citizens with a guaranteed basic income. You may have heard of this concept under several different names, including: Universal Basic Income, Basic Income Guarantee, Basic Living Stipend, or even Basic Living Demogrant. In this chapter we'll use the term *Universal Basic Income* (or UBI for short).

Although the detail of the UBI concept can vary, the idea behind it is to have governments provide all of its citizen with an income that would allow them to live, pay their bills and avoid becoming destitute.

The concept of UBI was first proposed by Sir Thomas More in his satirical work *Utopia*.[1] Published in 1516, it unsurprisingly coincides with one of the most transformative technological, political and economic eras of the Western civilization: the Renaissance. The idea gained favour once more in the late 1700s, another period of transformation and transition, most notably by way of British human rights champion Thomas Spence and American revolutionary Thomas Paine. UBI bubbles up to the surface once more in the late 19th and 20th centuries, as industrialization of Europe and North America begins to alter the economic fabric of society, most notably with Karl Marx, Clifford Douglas, Bertrand Russell, Dennis Milner all in their own way, arguing in favour of its virtues.

Two insights should immediately jump out. The first is that the notion of universal basic income is nothing new. The second is that the subject seems to come up whenever the economy is in the process of undergoing radical and disruptive change. Now that it's being talked about once more, it signals that we are living in equally disruptive and transformative times. At the core of this transformation lie three distinct but connected technologies: machine learning, smart automation and artificial intelligence.

If you are worried, you should be. Every one of us should feel a shiver at the thought of being replaced by a machine, and becoming unemployed and having our professional opportunities taken away from us. We don't say this because we want you to feel miserable and scared, but because, if this threat is something you care enough to worry about, you will be all the more likely to transition from worrying to taking action. This book is about equipping you with as much knowledge and insights as you need to do exactly that.

Preparing for the new paradigm

Looking at advances in technology in the last few years, it isn't all that difficult to see how new business solutions such as machine learning, smart automation and artificial intelligence *could* decimate the white-collar workforce in the way that machine shop and manufacturing automation decimated the blue-collar workforce. Note our use of 'may' and 'could' rather than 'will'. We don't have a crystal ball. We don't know what will happen. We don't know how companies, workers, legislators and educators will manage this shift. We don't know how quickly they will all adapt to this new paradigm and evolve to meet its challenges and turn threat into opportunity. What we do know, however, is that the more agile you are, and the quicker to adapt, the better your chances. Some will lose their jobs and never recover from that loss. Others will use this new wave of disruption to their advantage and come out ahead. The choice begins with a combination of awareness and will.

Awareness, initiative and resources: an adaptation playbook

The transformative impact of these shifts on the business world brings us to a fork in the road. On one side, you have these three technologies eliminating tens of millions of jobs over the next few decades. On the other, you have these three technologies enhancing tens of millions of human workers and making them more productive, more skilled, more effective and more valuable. These two paths exist simultaneously, and it is important to realize that whichever one you *initially* find yourself on may not be your choice. The one you *eventually* find yourself on, however, *is* your choice. If you remember nothing else from this chapter, this is the key thing.

Economic shifts like the one we are all about to experience have happened before. Early in the 20th century, the livery industry was annihilated by the invention of the motorcar. The electrification of cities killed off common professions like chimney sweeps and lamp-lighters. Improvements in manufacturing technologies spelled the end of knife sharpeners, the same way that the Internet put an end to door-to-door salesmen. Technology advancements always kill professions. It's nothing new. The question you have to ask yourself, is this: How did livery owners, chimney sweeps, lamplighters, knife sharpeners and door-to-door salesmen survive? Simple: they transitioned into other jobs – jobs that were actually in demand.

It wouldn't have been uncommon, for an astute livery owner who understood what was about to happen to their business to open up a service station and make the best of both worlds – whether both businesses remained profitable or one ended up replacing the other. It also wouldn't be all that uncommon to find a chimney sweep transitioning to mending roofs and repairing chimneys... . While certain jobs may be made obsolete by new technologies, the workers themselves don't *In the real world, survival belongs to the most adaptable.* have to be. Not if they can quickly evolve with them. *Survival of the fittest* is an overrated and misunderstood slogan. In the real world, survival belongs to the most *adaptable*.

In the example of a livery owner also catering to motorcars, that adaptability was predicated on three things:

- *awareness* of the impending threat;
- the *initiative* to turn threat into opportunity;
- access to the capital and *resources* needed to create a new business to take advantage of that change.

In the case of the chimney sweep and lamplighter, access to capital is more limited, but the same principles apply – *awareness*, *initiative* and *resources* form the core of their ability to evolve and transition:

Awareness that change is imminent and unstoppable is the catalyst for change.

The *initiative* to adapt and evolve is the catalyst for adaptation.

Access to *resources* is the toolkit that enables an individual to physically adapt to that change.

Initiative, we can only help you with to a point, but the chapters in this book should be motivation enough to give you the drive and energy you need to adapt. When it comes to awareness and pointing you to critical resources though, we have you covered.

Embracing technology partnerships and augmentation: none of this is about humans vs machines

You may have noticed that our focus throughout this book is squarely on making the most of human–machine partnerships, not on pitting humans against machines. We choose not to treat humans and machines as competitors because they don't have to be. They shouldn't be. From the most rudimentary plough to the most advanced supercomputer, machines should always be tools that enhance, augment and ultimately serve the needs of mankind. This is not solely a philosophical approach to the relationship between humans and machines but a practical one: pitting humans against machines is ultimately self-defeating, counterproductive and costly. Whatever short-term gains might be achieved in the effort will be eclipsed by the long-term costs.

In our view, the most productive and ultimately rewarding role of machines is to augment human capabilities. Machines can help us solve problems faster; transport us and freight quickly and safely, lift objects that we cannot; shape metal, build with concrete and steel; manufacture products quickly and with microscopic precision. Machines – intelligent or not – are, at their core, tools designed to solve practical problems and augment human capabilities. That age-old human augmentation role lies at the core of our perspective on how to adapt to technological change.

In order to understand how technological disruption can be an opportunity rather than a threat, ask yourself the most basic technological question of all: How does this technology help me? Or rather: How can I use this technology to *augment* myself?

A few examples:

- Can an AI tool or digital assistant help me save 45 minutes per day just by organizing and managing my schedule for me?
- Can an AI tool, digital assistant or bot help me save two hours per day by reading my e-mails, prioritizing them, replying to the ones requiring minimal attention, and keeping notifications and distractions to a bare minimum?
- Can an AI or smart automation tool save me hours of work by researching topics and generating reports and briefs for me?
- Can smart automation save me hours of work by autonomously creating quality presentations and reports?
- Can I use an AI or a small army of bots to save me hours of work by performing basic, repetitive, tedious tasks like filing expense reports, sending out e-mails and organizing conference calls and meetings?

Augmenting yourself towards becoming a more valuable worker

Insight: our research indicates that the principal reasons why companies usually invest in smart automation and transformative technologies are improved operational efficiency and the ability to scale quickly. Think about these objectives. Could you make the argument that an augmented workforce – one that leverages machine learning, smart automation and artificial intelligence to substantially increase its productivity and velocity, at scale, without incurring a proportional increase in man-hour costs – would satisfy the objectives stated above? Yes. You most certainly could. This means that, at the very least, *augmenting* human workers with smart technologies instead of outright *replacing* them with machines ought to be part of the conversation.

And if workforce augmentation is a legitimate adaptive strategy for companies to pursue within the scope of an economy on track to be transformed by machine learning, smart automation and artificial intelligence, then we need to talk about how workers can learn to augment themselves through technology, and how organizations can participate in that workforce transformation.

From white-collar and blue-collar jobs to next-collar jobs, and back again: what colour will the collars of tomorrow be?

You are probably aware of the difference between blue- and white-collar jobs: blue-collar jobs tend to be more of a manual-labour nature while white-collar jobs tend to be more akin to working in an office. A number of blue-collar jobs pay substantially better than many white-collar jobs, so don't make the mistake of assuming that white-collar jobs are necessarily higher-wage jobs, or that they require more advanced degrees. That often is the case, but the economics of white- vs blue-collar jobs are far more complex than the label we assign them.

To further complicate matters white- and blue- are not the only collar colour designations. *Pink-collar* refers to members of the service industry. *Grey-collar* refers to the types of skilled technicians – like engineers – who bridge the gap between white-collar and blue-collar jobs. (We will come back to the grey-collar designation in a moment.)

We bring this up for two reasons:

- First, we cannot tackle the topic of the future of work without drawing a clear distinction between the impact that machine learning, smart automation and artificial intelligence will have on blue- and white-collar jobs.
- Secondly, as blue-collar and white-collar jobs are impacted by technology, they may transform into entirely new categories of jobs with entirely new collar colour designations.

Thirty years from now, the binary, two-colour model we use to compartmentalize various types of work may no longer reflect the reality of the workplace.

As we explained earlier in the book, as technology worms itself into the day-to-day of white-collar work and blue-collar work, every worker will naturally become a technologist. As this change takes hold across industries, blue-collar and white-collar will likely merge into a broader ecosystem of grey-collar workers: technologists working with and alongside machines. The challenge for us is that grey-collar may be the wrong nomenclature for this, and most of the other colours are already taken. How then, do we describe the next generation of 'collars'?

It is important to realize that once the fog of technological disruption clears, and the technologist aspect of each job that survives this transition becomes mainstream, white-collar will still be white-collar, blue-collar will still be blue-collar, and the same will be true of orange-, gold-, black-, grey-, red- and green-collar jobs. Even if they end up looking and feeling very different from the types of jobs we grew up with, lawyers will still be lawyers, CEOs will still be CEOs, physicians will still be physicians, and teachers will still be teachers.

Will some jobs vanish completely? Perhaps, but most won't, and new jobs will emerge to serve new needs and solve new challenges. They always do. The trick is to keep swimming with the current and not fall behind.

Competing in a world of augmented workers and technologists: how professionals should leverage smart automation to increase their value

The challenge is to plot a course that will get us from here to there, even though 'there' is not all that well defined. Fortunately, while we may not be able to predict the future, we can anticipate the general direction of the next decade of technological advancements and investments. We have already brought up machine learning, smart automation and artificial intelligence, but we should also bring up a few more key technologies:

- The most obvious of these is the Internet of Things (or IoT). The ubiquitous connectivity of objects, devices and environments means that we will increasingly be interacting with our surroundings. Author and MIT Lab instructor David Rose delivers an interesting perspective in his book *Enchanted Objects* in which he predicts that smart, connected objects will increasingly feel more like magical objects than technology.[2] Two insights can be derived from this. The first is that connected, responsive, intelligent objects will increasingly surround us and bring new functionality to our everyday lives. The second is that, as these objects grow increasingly intelligent and capable, both the ease with which we interact with them and their value to us are bound to increase.

- Edge computing builds on Rose's predictions. If you aren't familiar with edge technologies, think of them as machine learning and AI migrating away from the cloud and to the network edge. What is the network edge? Devices. The short version: AI and machine learning increasingly living inside IoT devices as opposed to IoT devices having to connect to AI and machine-learning solutions in the cloud. The result: real-time, low-latency, localized AI and machine-learning capabilities. Edge technologies are what will progressively make IoT less about connectivity to the cloud and more about localized AI functionality. In Rose's thematic language, this means that enchanted objects will not merely be connected objects that exhibit enchanted-like functionality but truly smart objects.

- 5G – the new cluster of wireless technologies that combines new standards, frequencies, and modes of wireless transmission that will complement 2G, 3G and 4G, promises to vastly improve data transfer speeds and supercharge the IoT.

The combination of the IoT, edge and 5G is critically important because it will shape technology infrastructure investments between 2020 and 2030, and will serve as the springboard for both the next evolution of the IoT and whatever next generation wireless technology comes after 5G (presumably 6G).

What does all of this mean for workers looking to prepare for the next two decades? The answer is actually already within the IoT, edge computing, and new wireless connectivity standards. Primarily: real-time language processing will soon allow *voice* to replace keyboards as the chief mode of input for humans. This is good news, as it suggests that human–machine partnerships will soon feel much easier, more natural and intuitive than they have been until now. This will further reduce barriers of entry that may have prevented traditionally analogue workers from transitioning to a digital worker ecosystem in the past. Blue-collar and white-collar workers who may not consider themselves particularly tech-savvy may find it easier to either trade their old-economy jobs for new-economy jobs, or accelerate their evolution towards becoming augmented technologists with minimal friction or training.

It also means that it will be easier than ever before for workers hoping to remain competitive to build and demonstrate precisely the sort of added value that employers tend to look for: productivity, initiative and relevant competence.

A question arises. If it will soon be easier than ever for workers to interface with smart technologies and become more professionally agile, what will stop everyone from doing it? In theory, nothing. In practice, ourselves. Earlier in the chapter we talked about awareness, initiative and resources, and this is partly why: we anticipate that a significant number of workers at risk of being displaced will not become aware of these changes in time, or demonstrate the initiative needed to transition from old to new behaviours and skillsets. These workers will therefore find themselves unable to identify and leverage the resources at their disposal that would otherwise allow them to transition in synch with technology disruption. In other words, if nothing else, reading this book gives you an advantage over every worker in your industry who has not.

Just because new technologies make things easier doesn't mean that the majority of people will catch on or will be willing to give new modes of thinking a try. At least not until they become mainstream – by which time it might be too late for them to set themselves apart from other job applicants. The earlier you act on the opportunities offered by change, the quicker you can adapt and evolve, the more opportunities you will make yourself available to. We observed a parallel to this logic on the business side with regard to digital transformation: the most agile, quick to adapt companies – the ones that jumped on digital transformation the fastest – were, on average much more profitable, competitive, and likely to grow and thrive than companies that were slow to adopt new technologies or resisted digital transformation altogether.

Building your own next-collar job toolkit

Transitioning from old-economy jobs to new-economy jobs can't be as simple as waiting for voice interfaces to replace keyboards, or for machines to take over all of your most repetitive and commoditized tasks. You will have to do a little bit more work than that, especially in the beginning. (It will get easier as machine learning, smart automation and artificial intelligence become more ubiquitous in the workplace, but we aren't quite there just yet.) Until then, here are actions we can all take to begin preparing for the coming AI-driven economy.

1. Focus on adaptation, not technology

This may seem counterintuitive advice since so much of our discussion revolves around new technologies, but the most important characteristic of human workers in an AI-driven economy (and in transitional economies leading into it) will be adaptability. Here is why: technology is in a constant state of change. Business models, the way we live, the way we work, the way we collaborate, the way we consume, are in a constant state of change. While even we cannot predict accurately what new technologies and business models will emerge in the next few decades, we can predict with 100 per cent certainty that change is inevitable, and, therefore, that the ability to change quickly and efficiently is the most critical trait that every worker, decision-maker and organization must prioritize.

But, how do you learn to become adaptable? The same way you learn to do or become anything else:

- by identifying people and organizations that have done it well;
- by studying what they did to get there;
- by putting those lessons into practice and learning how to get good at it.

If that is too vague or abstract, remember our earlier insights on *awareness*, *initiative* and access to *resources*. This falls squarely into the initiative section. Individuals who do the work will have an advantage over those who don't.

2. In a world of automation, focus on being the most well-rounded human being you can be

Let us assume for a moment that the worst-case scenario involving machine learning, smart automation and artificial intelligence is realized: work automation results in humans being forced to compete against machines rather than humans and machines working together symbiotically. In such a world, how would humans make themselves more valuable to employers?:

a. by being better at performing tasks that machines are also able to perform;
b. by being better at performing tasks that machines are not well equipped to perform.

The answer is, of course, b.

What kinds of tasks are we talking about?

Tasks involving leadership, judgement, insight, creativity, abstract thinking, intuition, empathy, cultural awareness, motivation, collaboration, encouragement, courage, strategic vision, etc.

We recently chatted with Norm Judah, Microsoft's Worldwide Services CTO about this topic, and he highlighted the importance of human judgement in a world driven by smart automation, machine learning and AI. In his view, we are still a very long way from even the most sophisticated AI models being able to outperform humans when it comes to creative thinking, cultural awareness and judgement. As these types of traits and skills are critical to businesses' success, and machines, no matter how sophisticated they may be, are not well equipped to outperform humans, this seems like an obvious.

Moreover, if you can successfully demonstrate that the value of humans in an AI-driven economy (whether nascent or mature) lies in their ability to leverage these human traits and skills, then it stands to reason that human workers who can demonstrate *exceptional* judgement, creativity, empathy, intuition, awareness and vision will find themselves in very high demand, no matter how much machine learning, smart automation and artificial intelligence have infiltrated an organization's business processes.

The best strategy for human workers who don't want to be replaced by machines and smart automation may be to focus on what makes them better humans rather than on becoming better technology users. Becoming better technology users matters too, but it is a secondary consideration. Developing human skills and traits that cannot be replicated by machines is far more valuable.

One example Norm Judah shared with us points to the problem of bias in AI models (a topic covered in greater detail in Chapter 4). Essentially, the challenge is as follows: every AI model, whether from inception or over time through model drift, will be plagued with programmatic biases. Example: AI bias might manifest itself as a mortgage-loan AI solution that identifies college-educated 30-something couples as ideal candidates for a loan, while identifying 20-something single mothers with no college education as less than ideal candidates for a loan. The AI may therefore favour approving loans for college-educated couples while disproportionately denying loan applications from single mothers. In recent years, examples of AI bias have turned up in search engines, corporate hiring systems and law enforcement computer systems, raising concerns about AI's ability to identify, let alone correct its own programmatic biases. The answer, Judah, suggests is simple: don't take humans out of the equation.

AIs are limited when it comes to nuance, context, the detection of external biases, and judgement.

Humans are limited in the amount of data they can process. That's where machine learning, smart automation and artificial intelligence come in. AIs, for their part, are limited when it comes to nuance, context, the detection of external biases, and judgement. Combine humans and AIs though, and what you have is the perfect combination of processing power and judgement: a well-rounded and symbiotic human–machine partnership that has the highest probability of delivering optimal outcomes.

3. *Unless you are in a highly specialized role or a STEM field, familiarize yourself with a breadth of technologies and technology use cases rather than a narrow stack of specialized tools*

The quickest path to adaptability and agility is to become as versatile as possible, and in a business environment increasingly driven by machine learning, smart automation and artificial intelligence, that means becoming comfortable and at least moderately capable with as diverse a portfolio of technologies as you can.

This takes time and effort. Everything worthwhile does. Becoming comfortable with dozens of technologies you are likely to encounter in your profession is not all that difficult or challenging though – at least no more than learning how to knit bonnets and grow tomatoes. And yes, here is where the months and years spent learning a plethora of new skills comes in handy: if you can learn hundreds of trivial analogue skills with increasing ease and comfort, you can do the same with technology skills.

A few examples of things you can learn:

- how to use and customize business dashboards;
- how to use AR and VR goggles to play games, visualize 3D models, manipulate 3D models, and create or edit 3D objects;
- how to transition from keyboard search queries to voice search queries;
- how sensors and IoT technologies can be used to collect data in retail, industrial and public environments;
- how IoT technologies, edge computing, and wireless networks can be used to automate warehouses, production facilities and various business-critical systems;
- how VR, AR and frictionless payment systems are transforming retail;
- how to use as many analytics tools as you can get your hands on;
- how to build, deploy and/or customize bots;
- how to recruit IT resources into your business unit, then tasking them with showing you how to boost productivity, improve operational efficiency and drive your business development efforts.

If you *do* happen to work in a STEM field, the above advice applies to you as well. You may want to consider splitting your professional development efforts between pursuing a fluency in technologies and tools you employ every day and becoming comfortable with adjacent technologies which may, at some future point in time, intersect with your specialty. For example, researchers already comfortable with advanced data analytics tools may consider *also* becoming comfortable with 3D and mixed reality tools, in case data visualization and data manipulation move from keyboards and screens to the virtual space – which looks increasingly likely. Or dental technicians may want to become increasingly fluent with 3D scanning, 3D modelling and 3D printing solutions, as these technologies are increasingly moving production of surgical-grade dental implants, dentures and bridges out of specialized production facilities and into private practices.

Specific advice for key job categories

Let's look at a few additional avenues of AI-friendly professional development.

Senior executives, middle executives and decision-makers

LEARN TO FILL THE JUDGEMENT GAPS THAT WILL CONTINUE
TO LIMIT DATA ANALYTICS TOOLS
The technology solutions we use today to make sense of data are increasingly shifting from traditional analytics to *predictive* analytics – helping decision-makers model the *possible* and the *probable* outcomes of their decisions. In the long term, as machine learning, smart automation and artificial intelligence continue to improve, today's data *analytics* tools will become tomorrow's *prescriptive* management tools.

Today's data analytics *tools will become tomorrow's* prescriptive *management tools.*

The trap: many companies will put too much trust in the reliability of these AI-driven prescriptive models, and will be tempted to treat them as superior to human decision-making instead of using them as they are intended – as tools to help humans make more informed decisions.

Reality: no matter how advanced machine learning, smart automation and artificial intelligence get in the next 30 years, they will not develop better complex business decision-making skills than humans. Incomplete information and programmatic biases will continue to limit machines' ability to see the whole field. Additionally, they will always lack the context, nuance, instincts and critical thinking of humans. Companies that forget this, or fail to understand this reality, will find out the hard way just how costly that mistake can be.

The fix: adopt a human–machine partnership approach to solving it. If humans are limited in their ability to process vast amounts of data and crunch them quickly, humans can be exceptional at interpreting, validating, gauging meaningfulness and making sense of new information. What this means is that AI-driven analytics tools that might *appear* to threaten an organization's need for human decision-makers instead create an opportunity for machine-learning-savvy decision-makers to showcase just how important human judgement is to the process of making risky and complex business decisions. Therefore, the most important skillset for decision-makers who will soon share the stage with sophisticated predictive and prescriptive modelling solutions is the ability to inject judgement into AI-driven decision-making processes.

DEALING WITH NEW PARADIGMS OF UNCERTAINTY

Similarly, a new skill we have begun to pay particular attention to is the ability to deal better with 'grey' predictions and probabilities. A grey probability is a probability that cannot be immediately interpreted as black or white, especially by a machine. These kinds of predictions are not easily subjected to a good/bad or safe/unsafe binary interpretation.

Example: an analytics tool running predictive modelling software concludes that a particular course of action has a 70 per cent probability of success. A prescriptive AI solution programmed to interpret a better than 65 per cent prediction as 'very likely to succeed' may indirectly convert a 70 per cent success rate prediction into the suggestion of a 100 per cent success rate by prescribing a strategy it now rates as having a very high probability of success. A decision-maker untrained in understanding how to manage grey predictions could easily miss the nuance and simply become a human rubber stamp for the AI. A decision-maker trained in managing grey probabilities would be able to push back against the AI's recommendation, look for flaws in the input, analysis and prescription, and run the problem again until flaws and biases have been worked out of it. Alternatively, the same decision-maker might decide to dig deeper into the 30 per cent chance of failure aspect of the analysis, and uncover threats and opportunities that the AI failed to detect or fully understand.

This ability to identify, interpret and leverage nuance in data and analytics models *without* being paralysed by it will be one of the most important practical skills sought in people tasked with making complex, analytics-based decisions. Although this will most certainly require some degree of fluency with specific analytics and AI-based technologies, at the core this is not technology-based at all. It is a deeply human skillset, very much rooted in critical thinking: inquisitive, analytical, disciplined, bias-averse, sceptical, self-directed, self-monitored and self-corrective. This particular cluster of skills does not require a sophisticated practical understanding of technology.

Information workers

DATA VALIDATORS AND AI BIAS HUNTERS

For information workers, most of the above is relevant, but instead of focusing on the decision-making aspect of the human–machine partnership equation, information workers should focus instead on *validating* the data, predictive models and prescriptive models delivered to them by machine-learning algorithms. We tend to think of this function as *applied scepticism*, although some will prefer to associate it to *due diligence*. Here is our thinking on this: bias always exists in AI-driven models. Therefore, information workers should always operate under the assumption that the analytical models created by machines, no matter how sophisticated they may be, are tainted by bias. An information worker's job is to identify that bias and serve as a check against it.

Here is why this is important. It doesn't matter how sophisticated an AI is, or what heights of power and speed cognitive computing achieve: if computers cannot understand how they may be misinterpreting data, or cannot know what data sets or rules have been omitted in their analytics models, all of the technology investments in the world won't protect them – or us – from tainted or flawed analysis.

On the front end, the data must be accurate and properly compartmentalized. The sources of that data being used must be identified and validated. The context of that data must be translated into rules and logic that the algorithms can understand and properly apply to their analysis. Someone must also understand the problem being analysed well enough to work with technologist and AI interfaces to identify information gaps and missing data sets. (What other data should we be collecting? Where should it come from? Where should it not come from? What is the best way to collect it? How will we apply this additional data to our analytics model? How do we translate this into logic that computers will be able to apply properly?)

On the back end, the same questions happen in reverse. What data did we miss? What additional sources of data did we miss? Was this data flawed or compromised in any way? Did we collect this data incorrectly? Was this data applied or interpreted incorrectly? Did we fail to identify bias and logical problems when we created our models? Is bias compromising our results?

We might not go so far as to call the ability to detect bias in AI logic a 'soft skill', but we do feel that, at the very least, it is *soft-skill*-adjacent. Millions of years of evolution resulted in the human brain being exceptional at detecting both patterns and breaks in patterns. Even if we don't immediately understand precisely what the problem is, we can sense that a problem is there. For all their computing power and improving ability to think like humans, machines do not enjoy the benefit of those years of evolution, and are not as good at detecting subtle and contextual irregularities. This human ability is precisely why information workers will be essential to companies that rely on machine learning and artificial intelligence to provide their decision-makers with analytical, predictive and prescriptive insights.

In addition to identifying and eradicating bias in AI-driven models, information workers' jobs as data and insights validators will also fill insights gaps relating to all manners of human nuance, from providing deeper insights relating to behavioural analysis and psychology, to fine-tuning the analysis and projection of language, culture and empathy.

Blue-collar workers

TRANSITIONING FROM LOW-PAID MANUAL-LABOUR JOBS TO SPECIALIZED SMART-AUTOMATION OPERATOR JOBS

You don't have to be an expert in technology, manufacturing or labour issues to understand just how devastating the automation of manual labour has been to blue-collar jobs. Depending on the function, the equipment and the efficiency of the process, a production facility can lower costs and deliver efficiency gains ranging from 2x to 30x simply by automating repetitive, manually-intensive processes. Machines may have higher upfront costs than that of a new human hire, but they usually quickly pay for themselves in higher productivity gains, quality improvements and lower operating costs. As a result, blue-collar workers were the first to be displaced en masse by automation, and this trend is not likely to stop any time soon.

If you are a blue-collar worker, you already know this. It may be your main reason for reading this book. If you are a blue-collar worker, you do have options, and the age of smart automation could bring about more opportunities for your career than threats. We refer you back to our earlier discussion about the importance of *awareness* and *initiative*. The difference between blue-collar workers who thrive in the coming economy and those who don't is disproportionately predicated on awareness and initiative. If you can visualize clear paths to career adaptation and take the initiative to pursue these paths, you will have a significantly higher chance of not being replaced by a machine than blue-collar workers who either cannot or choose not to.

THREE TRACKS FOR BLUE-COLLAR WORKERS HOPING TO SURVIVE
THE NEXT WAVES OF AUTOMATION

There are three options for today's blue-collar workers in the age of machine learning, smart automation and artificial intelligence: choose a blue-collar career that cannot be easily automated; change careers; or learn to work with (not against) automation. Let's go through them in order:

1　Blue-collar jobs that cannot be easily automated tend to be non-geofenced jobs (jobs that require workers to function outside of controlled, consistent, predictable environments like factories or industrial plants), jobs that require lifting, carrying and delivering heavy objects to an infinite number of possible destinations with unpredictable or otherwise complex terrain, working in environments that require a high degree of real-time improvisation, and working in remote areas where machines would either struggle to match human efficiency or incur higher costs than using human labour. Painting and performing maintenance and repairs on complex structures like suspension bridges and the Eiffel Tower, for instance, are the sorts of jobs that cannot be easily automated or mechanized. Carrying windows from a truck bed to a house under construction over uneven surfaces, in mud and dirt, over stairs and makeshift platforms, while negotiating countless permutations of obstacles like stacks of materials, piles of debris and makeshift workstations, is a job best left to human workers rather than robots. There are jobs out there that will not soon be made obsolete by robots or machines.

2 Changing careers is the second option, but that transition doesn't have to be all that radical. Blue- and black-collar job skills transfer exceptionally well to green-collar jobs, for instance. We don't want to fall into the trap of prognosticating the growth of green-collar jobs over the next few decades. No one really knows the true extent to which governments and industry will invest in green technologies and workers. Having said that, the green sector may very well drive the next energy and infrastructure booms. Once again, initiative will favour the bold: the first waves of blue- and black-collar (oil, coal and mining) workers to transition into green-collar (eco-focused) industry could benefit from their initiative to abandon dying careers for emerging ones.

Blue- and black-collar job skills transfer exceptionally well to green-collar jobs.

3 Learning to work *with* automation – or surrounded by it. Some of the most interesting examples of human–machine partnerships can already be found in manual-labour environments, and we expect that as businesses learn to appreciate the degree to which such partnerships are often preferable to full automation, they will become more prevalent across a broad swathe of industries, as described below.

Virtual reality, augmented reality and mixed reality   We can already see how virtual-reality, augmented-reality and mixed-reality solutions are being leveraged in industrial and labour-intensive industries to train, guide and augment human workers. A human worker equipped with VR goggles can learn how to assemble or test a complex part, for instance, or learn to perform complicated tasks faster and more cost-effectively than on a physical assembly line or in a machine shop. Once trained, that same human worker equipped with an AR/MR headset or goggles can be guided by an AI or specialized software to perform complex sets of similar tasks with minimal additional training and with consistent precision. Introduce additional layers of IoT sensors, sophisticated facilities mapping, and part-tracking solutions, and you can help a human worker visualize in real time how the industrial environment he or she evolves in is reacting to his or her needs, and how to optimize workflows.

These new visualization capabilities can be used at workstations by line workers tasked with specialized product assembly as well as by operations managers needing to get a larger view of a plant's systems in real time. They can also be used by maintenance technicians looking to access a building's structural blueprints, pinpoint the exact location of buried utilities, run diagnostic tests on electrical or hydraulic systems, or identify malfunctioning switches or valves along miles of wires or pipes.

Exoskeletons and human augmentation robotics   Another promising area of human–machine partnerships in this environment focuses on physical augmentation through mechanical exoskeletons and wearable load-bearing mechanisms. While these technologies are not finding their way into industrial environments as quickly as augmented-reality solutions, the ability to allow human workers to lift heavy loads using natural body motions offers promising opportunities in areas where forklifts may not always be ideal, and where more operational flexibility is often required. A mechanical exoskeleton that allows a human worker to pick up a half-ton crate or part, and walk it over to a workstation, shelf or truck bed, can be far more cost-effective and operationally efficient than the alternative of using cumbersome forklifts or operationally limited belt-driven systems to perform the same task.

One of the themes we kept running into while doing our research for this book is the importance of designing technology solutions for the edges. While 'designing for the edges' can mean different things to different people, one interpretation applies to mechanical exoskeleton solutions. This is a technology that naturally finds its place on the edges of industrial automation and mechanization.

Transitioning from a traditional forklift-operating function to operating an exoskeleton instead may not be the worst career move for blue-collar workers. Good places to start learning about exoskeletons and learn to operate them are Lockheed Martin, Honda, Ekso Bionics, Cyberdyne, Panasonic and Raytheon.

Before we move on, we should probably mention that exoskeletons can already be broken up into several different categories:

- full-body power suits (as above);
- 'supernumerary' robotic arms (think of these as robotic third or fourth arms);
- load-neutralizing tool-holding exoskeletons (to help human workers hold, carry, and brace heavy tools);
- powered gloves (that provide more strength and control to hands in precise and fatigue-inducing gestures);
- load-reducing back braces and supports;
- chairless chairs (which allow human workers to 'sit down' on lightweight exoskeletons worn over work clothes that lock in place whenever they need to sit down).

While all of these exoskeleton categories will enhance human capabilities and improve productivity, the category that provides the most long-term value for blue-collar workers looking to survive the advance of automation in industrial environments is the full body power suit. It is the category with the highest learning curve and potential for deep specialization and certifications.

Transitioning to maintenance, repair and systems management roles Another option for blue-collar workers is to transition into grey-collar functions like maintenance, repair and operations management. All machines need to be maintained and repaired, calibrated, customized and upgraded. While smart automation can already easily handle the synchronous and real-time operation of complex automation in industrial environments, some functions still fall to human workers to handle. The more machines take the place of human workers, the more opportunities for repair specialists and maintenance technicians will arise.

Retail workers

Our advice for retail workers isn't as involved as it is for other categories. The reality of machine learning, smart automation and artificial intelligence's impact on retail is that retail will increasingly become more frictionless, fluid and customer-centric. As the convenience of mobile commerce continues to eat into bricks-and-mortar shopping experiences and grow demand for delivery services, retailers will naturally consolidate around digital and virtual experiences, making bricks-and-mortar experiences more of a brand experience play rather than a true volume play. What this means for retail workers is that their industry is likely to shrink and simultaneously become far more connected and automated than it has been. As digital and physical experiences merge into this single, frictionless experience, retail customers will expect to be able to transition from online searches and app-based shopping to visits to physical stores to get their hands on a product for further inspection, pick up purchases, return purchases or engage in impulse purchases. Who they are, including their purchasing habits, transaction history and preferences, will have to be effortlessly integrated into their bricks-and-mortar experiences in a way that enhances the value of their visits and nudges them towards purchases but without being creepy, pushy or intrusive. While machine learning, smart automation and artificial intelligence will handle most of the computing – analysis, customer profile generation, predictive analytics, marketing messaging, timing and push, and prescriptive insights – it will be up to retail staff to convert these insights into pleasant and ultimately productive outcomes. Doing this properly will require a complex blend of professionalism, nuance, tact and charm that machines are not yet equipped to mimic or deliver on their own.

While the model we just described lends itself more easily to premium retail experiences, the opportunity to democratize premium retail experiences by using machine learning, smart automation and artificial intelligence shouldn't be lost on more mainstream and high-volume retailers. The ability to understand customer behaviours and their needs through smart analytics is, in and of itself, a potent tool for differentiation. This is especially true in an economy that strives to commoditize each and every retail transaction.

What was true before the Internet and machine learning found their way into retail will still be true when most retail experiences are reduced to a swipe and a tap: customer experiences matter. Customers *will* pay a premium (however small it may be) for friendlier customer service, smoother checkouts, faster deliveries, unexpected extra care, trust, confidence and security. At the very least, these differences will inform their preference.

If every retailer uses the same tools to transact online with customers, key differentiators for competitors, aside from the products themselves, eventually come down to three factors: price, a nexus of availability and delivery, and user experiences. In-store experiences therefore become the most fluid battle-ground and that is where retail workers can tip the scales either against their employers or in their favour.

In closing

The principles outlined above are industry-agnostic. You can apply them to every job. If you happen to be an accountant and worry about machine learning, smart automation and artificial intelligence eventually taking over your profession, be among the first in your market to leverage these technologies to augment your existing capabilities (or simply scale them without hiring new staff), and start focusing on injecting more customer care and personal touches into your professional relationships to increase their value to customers, partners and stakeholders. If you happen to be a physician or healthcare professional with an outpatient practice, be among the first in your market, hospital or group to leverage machine learning, smart automation and artificial intelligence solutions to automate tedious tasks (from appointment-scheduling to record-keeping); capture more patient data to create a more effective health monitoring and analysis practice; empower patients to use sensors, apps and data analytics tools on their own to better help you help them; and rely on prescriptive solutions to identify potential problems *and* treatments you might not have otherwise considered.

Your toolkit, no matter what industry you happen to work in today, and regardless of your job, is exactly the same: awareness, initiative, resources.

The resources are out there. Human workers looking to learn about new technologies can do so at little or no cost by using search engines to identify and access sources of information ranging from videos, news articles, white papers and infographics to user guides, training manuals and demonstrations. Training in the use of these new technologies can be a little trickier, but depending on where you happen to live, training programmes may be offered at little to no cost. From least to most expensive: if your current employer does not yet offer the kind of training you are looking for, talk to HR about either creating that training or helping you gain access to it. If your employer is not helpful, reach out to professional organizations and see if they can help you. If they are not helpful either, reach out to technology providers directly, and ask about any training and acclimatization programmes that might be available to you.

A wonderful example of a technology company making this kind of resource available to the public is Amazon. In late 2018, the retail and machine-learning giant opened dozens of its machine-learning courses to the public, for free, and threw in some certification paths for good measure. Look for these opportunities, whether they are offered by major tech companies like Amazon, Microsoft, IBM, Google and Salesforce, or through less conspicuously obvious smart automation, AI, machine learning, VR and IoT companies like Raytheon, Dassault Systèmes, GE or Disney.

If none of that bears fruit or meets your individual needs, you may need to reach out to trade schools and technical colleges in your area to see what options they offer or look for online courses and certifications. Some transitions will be easier than others. We acknowledge that change is hard, and that learning new skills can be a hurdle for anyone. Time, money, attention are all in short supply these days. We don't want to make this all sound easy or trivial. What we also know is that the time and effort you invest in learning how to use new technologies and better partner with machines offer the highest probability of job security and career agility in the coming decades. The more time and effort you invest in this now, the more opportunity you are likely to enjoy when machine learning, smart automation and artificial intelligence begin to replace human workers at a much higher rate of speed than they do now.

Your best bet is to become a more valuable human partner to the machines that surround you.

If it also wasn't already abundantly clear, we cannot stress enough the importance of soft skills in a world of mechanical efficiency. We keep repeating it for two reasons. First, because it is easy to fall back into daily technology-skills-acquisition anxiety. Just reading the previous paragraph probably shifted your focus back towards needing to acquire as many new technology skills as possible, as quickly as possible. When we do that, we tend to forget about just how vital the development of human skills and traits is to thriving in a world of smart automation. Being a better machine operator is not enough to bring value to an organization for the same reasons that being a better stylus operator doesn't make you a more valuable graphic designer. It is easy to forget that, so don't. In a world of automation, your best bet is to become a more valuable human partner to the machines that surround you. The second reason is that without human partners to guide, lead, adjust, motivate, inspire, protect, interpret, articulate, ponder, investigate, double-check, teach, judge and decide, smart automation will never produce the kinds of outcomes that the organizations that rely on it hope for and expect. In what may seem like a counterintuitive twist of irony, humans *are* the key to making smart automation work, especially in the next several decades. So-called 'soft skills' that were once scoffed at by those of us who looked with little favour on liberal arts degrees and humanities in general are going to be far more professionally valuable in a world of smart automation than they have been in the last century. Chief among them is leadership. If leadership was already important before all of this, it will become more critical than ever in a world of commoditized, repetitive, automated tasks.

CHAPTER SIX

How educational institutions should prepare for the next age of human–machine partnerships

Leaving 20th-century education behind

Every conversation we have with educators, business leaders and technology disruptors about the future of education and job training brings us to a common and almost universally shared insight: in order to start meeting the demands of a digitally-powered, AI-driven economy, education and job training are going to have to change. To be clear, we don't mean incremental change. The consensus is that the type of change that will be required to make education and job training relevant into the next few decades is radical. General consensus among educators and business leaders is essentially that we can address neither the educational nor the job training needs of an AI-driven future by holding on to models of education and training that were put in place at the start of the 20th century.

When today's Western-style primary and secondary education systems were originally put in place, chimney sweep, knife sharpener, livery boy, coal miner and lamplighter were still common occupations. Radio, television, the automobile and mechanical flying machines existed only in the fancy of science fiction writers like Jules Verne and HG Wells, to say nothing of computers, telecommunications satellites, mobile phones and intelligent computers. And yet, as we prepare to enter the second quarter of the 21st century, and already see how smart automation and the future of human–machine partnerships promise to radically change the nature of employment (and consequently the purpose of education and job training), we still cling to models of education and skills acquisition originally devised by people who could not have conceived of the Internet, mobile phones, the IoT and smart environments.

The change required to make education and job training relevant is radical.

Separating education and job training: practical considerations

1. Education *and* job training *do not serve the same function*

The simplest way to articulate the difference between education and job training is to think of *education* as a process by which students learn to become competent generalists, while *job training* is a process by which competent generalists learn to become competent specialists.

Any educational and job training ecosystem that fails to clearly define the difference between these two functions, and does not design both to perform the proper function, will not succeed in developing the types of citizen and workers we need in an AI-driven digital economy. Unless we correct this problem, the societal and economic impact of these failures will only grow worse.

How then, can we rethink (or at least adapt) 20th-century education and job training models for 21st-century needs?

2. When successive incremental improvements to an obsolete system are no longer enough: the case for rebooting education

Every product, organization, business model and system must, at some point in its lifecycle, reinvent itself. Everything becomes obsolete eventually, even ideas, and in this regard, education is no different. Sooner or later, trying to make old ideas and old systems continue to work in a world that has already moved on from 20th- and 19th-century methods, simply isn't going to work. So how does education move forward?

At its core, rethinking education and job training for a new age of human–machine partnerships is no different from any other engineering, economic or social problem.

Whether or not we allow intelligent computers to help us design a new educational model (and we probably should), we need to begin the process. This starts with a discussion about which fundamental aspects of education and job training matter, which ones don't, why and how each should either be replaced or adapted to the entirely new set of future needs.

One all too common mistake made by school systems that have not yet separated education and job training is the budgetary prioritization of educational topics deemed more easily convertible into practical job-critical skills (like science and maths) at the expense of others (like history, civics, literature and art), particularly when budget cuts require them to start making cuts to their educational resources. The underlying argument when these cuts are made is always that these topics matter less to future workers than science and maths. While we understand the economic and ideological forces behind this type of rationalization, we feel that it is counterproductive. Removing creativity, emotional interpretation, artistic expression and cultural history from a child's curriculum robs them of the very foundations they need to one day become prolific creative think-ers, problem-solvers and insightful decision-makers. Aside from the value to society of consistently raising generations of rational, capable, emotionally evolved adults, these also happen to be the very qualities that employers are increasingly desper-ate to find in their new hires. One key reason for this is that these dimensions of knowledge, understanding, contextualiza-tion and insight are critical to complex problem-solving and responsible, ethical decision-making. For human–machine part-nerships to be successful, particularly as they relate to decision-making, the human element of those partnerships must have these abilities built in. If we fail to teach tomorrow's workforce these essential skills, we will have failed in our most basic educa-tional duties.

Secondly, from a purely practical standpoint, how can we expect to some day be able to teach intelligent computers and smart environments to mimic human problem-solving skills and empathy, to say nothing of being able to properly identify users' moods, emotions and needs, if tomorrow's tech profes-sionals have been robbed of the very education they need in order to fully understand these cues and their meaning themselves?

Long before debates about education become about ideol-ogy, political agendas, personal beliefs (or even budgets), the fundamental problem that governments and educational systems face today is the fact that they are grossly ill-adapted to produce the kinds of workers and technology users the world will need in the next few decades. Primary and secondary schools are still trying to prepare young adults for 20th-century industrial economies rather than 21st-century post-industrial economies, and no amount of tinkering and technology patches (like 'computer class') will fix that. What we need is an entirely new model of education, and a parallel model of professional skills development and job training: a 'reboot', in 21st-century parlance.

3. Rebuilding education from the ground up: letting form and purpose define function

Let's pretend that we have been tasked with redesigning education and job training from scratch, for the era of AI-augmented human–machine partnerships. Forget traditional K-12 and P-12 (pre-school, primary and secondary education up to age 16–17) programmes. Forget how elementary and secondary education have been structured until now. If we could start all over, what would education designed for 2030 and beyond look like?

It isn't enough to consider the topics and substance of education and job training. We also have to consider the form that teaching and training will take: what environments and conditions are ideal to minimize distractions and maximize retention? Would classrooms still look the way they do, with rows of chairs and desks facing a teacher's desk and a whiteboard? Should they perhaps instead be rearranged in a semicircle, to favour discussion and debate between students, and keep their device screens more private? Should desks be arranged in small clusters that favour teamwork? Should we instead return to more classical teaching theatres, with their semi-circular rows of seats overlooking a stage-like lecture floor?

What about eliminating classrooms altogether? Should schools attempt to emulate modern workspaces, with their open floor plans, creative spaces, individual thinking pods and soundproofed meeting rooms?

How might class size and seating schemes impact social interactions and class participation? How might these changes help teach students the types of collaboration, leadership and creative problem-solving skills they will need later in life? Considerations like these are not trivial. Before we begin to actively fold job training into an educational curriculum, we must incorporate elements of job training into our new shared educational experience. By introducing what are usually referred to as 'soft skills' into our new teaching model, we can help better prepare students for the professional world.

4. Elementary education in the age of magical objects: teaching children to find the right balance between analogue and digital tools

Now, we come to subjects: history, biology, algebra, literature. Tear it all down and start over. What do we really need to teach? What really matters? Forget teaching to the test. Forget what you think children and young people need to study in order to tick the right boxes on a university application form. Start over.

Starting at the beginning, teaching children how to draw, and paint, and glue things together, then read and write when they are young still matters. None of that should change; if anything, what we should do is add a little more to it. Building on those skills, the next step might be to incorporate more human–machine interactions into the classroom experience, such as being around robots and AI interfaces. Teach how to use common types of human–machine interfaces from touchscreens to voice-activated software. The idea is to teach them how to navigate a world filled with smart objects (or in child-friendly parlance, *magical objects*).

We're not suggesting that analogue forms of creativity, manual dexterity and craft-based skills should be replaced by digital versions of them. Quite the contrary: children still need to under-stand real, tactile, analogue spatial relationships and real-world cause and effect. Errors in the real world cannot be deleted like they can on a screen or in a virtual space, and that lesson is too important to scratch from their development, even by a fraction.

Care should also be taken not to favour digital solutions over analogue ones. The proper approach should not be ideological (example: 'human–machine partnerships are superior to analogue do-it-yourself hands-on solutions') but functional. Children should be taught the value of evaluating different types of approaches to solve a problem, and ask themselves when a human–machine partnership is appropriate and when it is not. For instance: *Is this a problem that requires scissors or a 3D printer?* Or *Is this a problem I should work out myself or should I rely on an AI to think it through for me?*

This means that we will have to create an entirely new system of values for children, particularly with regard to their relationship with technology. At the heart of this system probably lies the need to achieve a sense of balance. By this we mean that from an early age, children must learn the risks of leaning too much or too little on digital solutions. We want to help them learn to love every tool in their toolkit, so that when the time comes for them to start solving problems for themselves, they will be equipped to do so in their own way. Many will opt for the easiest and most frictionless solution; having the confidence and the knowledge that come with knowing how to solve analogue problems on their own will go a long way towards helping them find fulfilment in their lives, and developing more effective and ultimately more satisfying human–machine partnerships in the future.

It's also not a bad idea to teach programming to very young children. Programming may take on a far more fluid and frictionless form in a world increasingly powered by AI solutions, so we don't necessarily mean 'computer programming' in the way that it is taught today. What we *are* suggesting is that, because human–machine partnerships will continue to insinuate themselves into our everyday lives, teaching young children how to program machines (and communicate with them as programmers, not just users) from an early age makes a lot of sense.

Aside from the purely tactical aspects of adapting education to the impending age of AI-assisted everything, it is imperative that we help children develop into capable, self-sufficient, critical thinkers with practical analogue skills in parallel to a new portfolio of human–machine partnership skills. The last thing we want to do is create a generation divided between a technology-averse working class that has trouble adapting to constant technological change, and a privileged class of dull little masters who rely so much on machines to answer questions and solve problems for them that they become essentially useless. We must strike for balance. In other words, we must work to develop successive generations of hybrid technologists who will be equally comfortable operating in analogue environments and AI-driven ones.

5. Designing secondary education environments, experiences and methodologies for an AI-driven economy

The idea isn't to replace one thing with another, and we don't advocate the elimination of so-called 'non-essential' or 'low-priority' subjects from school curricula. While the argument could be made that science and maths are more useful to future technologists than literature and history, we find the premise dubious. (See our argument in defence of the liberal arts a little further on in this chapter.) In our view, education tends to work better when it is more additive than subtractive, and richer in subjects than poorer in them. Education's aim should be to produce well-rounded individuals, not narrowly-educated ones.

Education should be designed to deliver a wide breadth of knowledge, experiences and skills, while job training should focus on delivering a depth of practical experiences and skills that will equip individual beneficiaries to grow into capable experts.

Rebooting education requires that more, not fewer, subjects be incorporated into primary and secondary education systems. But how can this be done when school schedules are already so full? By focusing on what works and trimming the fat from what doesn't. For instance, what lessons from business environments can we apply to classroom environments? Here's one suggestion: in the business world, 30-minute meetings are often more effective than hour-long meetings, so why don't we cut some class times down from one hour to half an hour? We aren't suggesting that all periods be reduced from one hour to 30 minutes, but just as some meetings don't need to last a full hour, some classes also could stand to take up less space in a student's day.

Earlier in this chapter, we proposed that schools could learn from corporate environments' experimentation with rearranging and adapting different types of spaces for their workers: open collaborative spaces, meeting rooms, individual thinking pods. This is where schools can rethink their floor plans and how students are seated in their classrooms. Why not treat student–teacher interactions at a school more like co-worker/employee/manager interactions at most companies?

Rebooting education requires that more, not fewer, subjects be incorporated into primary and secondary education systems.

With these changes also come entirely new layers of challenges. For instance, how do you ensure that, in the age of digital assistants, bots and AIs, homework assignments (like research papers) are actually done by a live student as opposed to a digital surrogate? How do you protect the integrity of a school's testing ecosystem in the age of hacking and compromised cybersecurity? AI-powered solutions will likely have to be developed to flag these types of infractions, but this only helps illustrate that for all the potential benefits that progress brings, it also drops its share of challenges and problems on our doorstep. These unintended consequences too, must be thought through.

6. *Remote learning, mixed reality and AI: how to use digital technologies to enrich and broaden the meaning of 'presence' in educational environments*

The educational model we have described is adaptable to remote learning. We recognize that as digitization continues its physical growth and social communications become more frictionless, the percentage of students attending schools remotely is certain to grow. Equipping all teaching spaces with screens, cameras and microphones and mixed-reality equipment that will allow distant students to participate in a lecture, class or project, is a given.

It is also likely that some combination of mixed-reality technologies will be used to enhance those students' experience, if only to make them feel less 'apart' from their educators and classmates. Whether this takes on the form of virtual avatars or holographic projections (or nothing at all) remains to be seen, but the prospect of making remote students more present in a physical space they cannot occupy is intriguing and filled with potential. We have already begun to see examples of how virtual-reality and augmented-reality experiences can be easily integrated into education, and how much educational promise they may yet hold. ClassVR, launched in 2017, is a company already seizing on this opportunity by providing VR headsets, curriculum-aligned content, training, support and guidelines for educators looking to develop VR-augmented lesson plans. The company is already working with teachers and students in the United States, Australia, the United Kingdom, China and the Middle East, and is likely to be joined by other companies understanding the business potential for virtual-reality technologies in education.

The world of mixed-reality technologies may even hold the key to shortening certain classes in length, and the importance of rethinking how schools and classrooms should be designed.

What are the implications of mixed-reality technologies when applied to individual learning:

- Does a teacher have to be present to teach students about the inner workings of a human cell if the lecture can be delivered by way of a VR headset and accompanying audio explanation?
- Does a teacher have to be present (and/or engaged) if these same students have access to an AI already trained to answer questions about the lecture?

What might that teacher be free to do during that time? Grade papers? Work with another group of students engaged in an experiment or hands-on project? Prepare a lab for yet another team of students?

Students will have the physical ability to personalize and customize their own curricula if they so wish. The only question is to what extent their schools and school systems will allow them to do so. Barring a myopic and regressive (not to mention short-lived) bureaucratic response from recalcitrant educational institutions, this capability, made possible through a fairly uncomplicated type of human–machine partnership, could enable primary and secondary educational systems to deliver precisely the type of breadth in educational experiences and opportunities that we referred to earlier in this chapter. Imagine having the option to learn German from (at least in part) a native speaker. Imagine having the option to learn music appreciation from (at least in part) some of the best music experts in the world. Imagine being able to go to school and learn anything you are interested in from any number of experts from around the world, in your time, at your leisure, and in an environment that encourages that kind of curiosity and thirst for knowledge. Technology and a reboot of education can make that possible.

Technologies open an entirely new world of possibilities for students dealing with a range of special needs. Whether a student wrestles with learning disabilities, mobility issues, or any challenges that traditional education hasn't been able to properly address, virtual reality, augmented reality, remote collaboration and AI technologies can be readily adapted to help students find solid ground upon which to compete against their less challenged peers. This particular area of assistive use for maturing digital technologies becomes particularly important once you realize that more than 1 in 10 public school students in the United States lives with a disability.[1]

In addition to allowing teachers to free themselves from some lectures, and allowing remote students to attend classes virtually, mixed-reality technologies and remote meeting solutions can *also* be used by a school to teach a subject even if that school doesn't have an in-house resource that actively teaches that class. For instance, if you are a gifted high-school student who wants to take a class in microbiology, but you live in a school district that doesn't offer that option in 2005, that would have been a problem. In 2025, it may not be. In 2035, it certainly won't. Once schools begin more broadly to adopt mixed-reality and remote-attendance technologies, students will be able to attend classes and lectures from virtually anywhere that offers an Internet connection and a gateway interface into the class itself.

We don't believe that virtual teaching experiences and AI will replace teachers altogether. We don't believe that replacing teachers with machines and pre-recorded lectures is an effective educational model. Teachers still need to bring students together around a topic, inspire, motivate, foster discussions, and act essentially as a 'manager' and patron for their student teams. And so, while human teachers *could* some day be replaced by machines, we believe that they should not. Human teachers are and should always be the beating heart of education. Having said that, a combination of teacher–machine partnerships and student–machine partnerships could very well deliver an entirely new era of education, and one perfectly suited for an AI-driven world.

6. *Essential new subjects for the digital age*

As to which new categories of subjects should be taught alongside literature, science, maths, art and languages, a short list of topics to consider adding to middle school and high school may usefully include:

- fact-checking;
- ethics;
- privacy and digital security;
- applied programming;
- working with AI;
- virtual modelling;
- remote collaboration;
- applied leadership;
- game theory.

Some of these subjects may require as much of a time commitment as traditional subjects, while others could be taught and revisited in small doses and at regular intervals. (Ethics and fact-checking, as crucial as they may be, may not require a daily class. Programming and virtual modelling, probably do.) Ultimately, what these subjects need to be remains a question mark, but educators, business leaders and lawmakers need to start having this discussion.

7. Economic considerations

We are aware that the reboot of education cannot be achieved unless schools and the systems that fund them get serious about properly investing in education. We find ourselves on familiar ground: several years ago, when businesses around the world were only beginning to feel the effects of technology disruption, the vast majority of executives were sceptical about the need to prepare their organizations for what was coming, and reluctant to devote precious resources to sweeping digital transformation initiatives. We also remember rather vividly the sense of doom that digitally-savvy junior executives and forward-looking technologists conveyed to us whenever the subject of digital transformation and adaptation came up, especially when the companies being discussed were very large, very established enterprises that we would rather not name.

'This is too much too fast', was the general consensus. 'Ships this big don't turn on a dime', was another common response. 'This is going to force us to completely change our business model. They'll never go for it.'

Well, they went for it. Enterprise-sized ships may not turn on a dime, but adjust course they did, and in well under a decade, two-thirds of businesses in North America and Western Europe managed to transform themselves into competitive, digitally-capable 21st-century companies. That process is still ongoing, and as digital transformation eventually settles into predictable cycles of digital adaptation, the evolution of business organizations towards an AI-driven world should continue without too much friction.

For roughly a third of businesses, however, the transition from old to new hasn't exactly gone very well so far, and their failure to adapt to new technologies, new business models and new ways of remaining competitive in their respective markets, threatens to make them obsolete.

School systems find themselves in a similar position as the business world did a decade ago. There are only three ways forward:

1 A thorough reboot of education, in keeping with the suggestions in this book.
2 Investments in technological patches that will equip schools with new technologies but won't address any of the other challenges that tomorrow's workforce needs schools to help them solve.
3 Do nothing, and hope things work out.

In 2018, K-12 teachers across the United States are protesting for better pay and adequate school funding. Listening to their stories, it is difficult to fathom how school systems with eroding budgets, an inability to provide enough textbooks, let alone chairs and desks for all of their students, and buildings falling into deeper states of disrepair year after year, can possibly transform themselves the way we have described. Yet, that is exactly what they are going to have to do.

Every country's educational system is, at its core, that specific country's employment pipeline. If that pipeline produces unemployable workers, this then creates friction via joblessness, stress and investor pessimism. If instead, that pipeline produces not only employable workers, but agile, adaptable workers who can easily plug into a complex and modern economy, that country is more likely to enjoy a dynamic economy driven by innovation, a can-do attitude and investor optimism. Like any system, how much you put in usually determines what you get back: adequate funding results in adequate outcomes. Sub-par funding results in sub-par outcomes.

You cannot build a first rate 21st-century economy without investing in a first-rate educational and job training pipeline. Just as it took many companies more time than others to realize that if they didn't take digital transformation seriously, they would no longer remain competitive, it may take some countries more time to come to terms with this basic reality than others. And just as the task of steering very large companies and their crushing bureaucracies towards radical change once seemed daunting, the task of steering very large countries towards radical changes in the way they invest in and manage education now seems daunting. But in the end, every ship is built to turn when it must, no matter how difficult it may be to fight its own inertia; and whether its crew is motivated by opportunity or desperation, it *will* turn because it must.

Every country's educational system is that country's employment pipeline.

New schools will replace old ones. New technologies will inevitably find their way into the hands of students. More efficient ways of teaching and preparing students for an economy filled with entirely new opportunities and challenges will replace outdated and inefficient ones. The system will adapt and evolve. And as it does, so will the funding to make this transformation happen. Even if we begin to see more cooperation between public education and private industry, which is a distinct possibility, the evolution of education is as inevitable as the evolution of businesses and the economies they operate in.

8. *Folding training into education: should universities rethink their role in this new ecosystem, and shift their focus from education to job training?*

We have already seen how aspects of job training – such as discipline-agnostic core competencies like computer skills, problem-solving, teamwork and collaboration with AI – naturally fit into a broad education curriculum. When the time comes to shift from delivering a breadth of knowledge and skills to a depth of practical, professional knowledge, the basic technical, administrative and critical thinking skills acquired over the course of 10 to 12 years of primary and secondary education should serve as a solid, adaptable and dynamic foundation upon which to build an effective job training – or *career preparation* – programme.

Here, we come to a fork in the road: should the world's universities function as educational institutions or professional schools? Should they either be one or the other? Could they realistically be both?

Remember our earlier premise: an *education* should train students to be competent generalists, while *job training* should train them to be competent specialists. Every economy, even one increasingly driven by AI, requires skilled, competent workers and decision-makers. No matter how many machines begin to replace these roles, the economy will still need humans to do most of these jobs, at least for the foreseeable future. And if not these specific jobs, other jobs that machines cannot perform as well (or at a sufficient scale to displace human workers entirely), or new jobs that will emerge from new types of human–machine partnerships. In short, no matter how many machines begin to perform tasks once performed by human workers, the need for skilled, competent human workers will not end any time soon, if ever. Ergo: the need for job training is unlikely to end as well.

This brings us back to our fork in the road: should universities focus on developing more highly-educated but professionally-unskilled citizens, or on developing highly-skilled professionals with marketable skills?

This is at the heart of the debate over the value of liberal arts universities (or programmes) vs the value of professional schools. Unless you are already financially independent, does it make sense to earn a degree in history or English literature when it would make more practical sense to pursue a professional degree in law, systems engineering, healthcare, business management or engineering?

This question is increasingly relevant, as automation and the expansion of the *gig economy* (part-time and full-time contractors replacing traditional employees) continue to steer hiring and contractor-selection decisions towards skilled specialists rather than unskilled generalists.

Perhaps a better way to ask the question might be to consider what ratio of highly-educated generalists to highly-skilled professionals would be ideal in a society (not just an economy) in which both *do* create value. While the value created by skilled specialists may be easier to measure and understand, we should be careful not to underestimate the value of thought leadership, academic expertise, creativity, cultural awareness and specialized knowledge that are the hallmarks of the beneficiaries of a liberal arts education. We caution that while it may seem expedient and logical to prioritize job training and career preparation over liberal arts degrees and the pursuit of higher education (at the expense of job training), we must resist

We must resist the urge to engineer a society entirely made up of skilled worker bees.

the urge to engineer a society entirely made up of skilled worker bees. A human society, and perhaps especially one increasingly reliant on machines and artificial intelligence to function, must continue to produce artists, philosophers, poets, thought leaders. Just as an economy is not limited to the stock market, a society is not limited to the economy. Artists and thinkers are indispensable to society, and we should both encourage and protect institutions and programmes that aim to attract, develop and empower them.

Having said that, while most people should be both free and able to pursue knowledge and whatever passions inspire them in their free time, perhaps the majority of higher education institutions should prioritize career preparation and job training. Does a society need artists and thinkers? Absolutely. But assuming that K-12 and P-12 school systems did their job properly, the foundations have been laid for every 20-something to know how to think and create. Ideally, it should not be a university's job to fill that fundamental kind of a role. What the world also needs is a pipeline of engineers, doctors, doers and makers, and universities are especially well equipped to help form them. Therefore, most universities should begin to think of their function perhaps more as professional schools than as 'institutions of higher learning'. Applying the 80/20 rule to this idea probably isn't a bad place to start.

The simplest way to look at this shift is to ask a university what types of graduates it is producing: is it sending professionals into the world, or merely graduates? In other words, what can these graduates do? Where do they go?

Medical schools produce healthcare professionals. Law schools produce legal professionals. Engineering schools produce engineers. Generally-speaking, professional schools produce competent, professional, specialized workers. Whether a professional training programme lasts eight weeks or eight years, its purpose is to create competent specialists with marketable and employable skills. If the educational system that prepared students for this phase of their functional development did its job, a balance can be struck between education (breadth of knowledge) and job training (depth of skills). For most members of a society in which more than full employment and individual productivity matter, this should be the goal of a joint but distinct education and training ecosystem.

9. *Looking to the private sector for new educational and job training opportunities: culture, values, methods and the future of private–public partnerships*

Putting aside in-house training programmes for a moment, what we are talking about here is an opportunity for large businesses with specific needs to partner with local and state governments in educational and job training ventures – namely programmes and schools capable of delivering unique, custom-designed tracks for future hires.

A technology company could co-fund *and* co-manage a school (or a programme within a school) that identifies, recruits and trains students with an aim of hiring them once they graduate. In fee-paying schools, this company could create mechanisms by which promising applicants might be sponsored through a combination of private and public scholarships. This type of endeavour could begin in secondary school and see itself extended into post-secondary school programmes, either at universities or professional schools specifically established to that end.

Take that idea a step further: imagine Google, Microsoft, or IBM or Apple, not only recruiting from top university programmes like MIT, the California Institute of Technology and Harvard, but *building* co-sponsored (and even company-branded) tracks *within* (or *in partnership with*) universities. These programmes could be used to do far more than just identify, attract and develop future hires. More importantly, these programmes could also be used to inculcate company culture, values and methods into future hires while they are still students.

This notion of creating university-like mechanisms to bake culture, values and methods into future professionals isn't new. Military academies and seminary schools pioneered the model centuries ago. In the mid-1950s and 1960s, the corporate world began to adapt the model, to its own needs, starting with Disney and McDonald's: Disney University (established 1955) and Hamburger University (established 1961) were designed to teach, form, develop and prepare employees for successful careers. Although not accredited like traditional colleges and universities, and certainly not embedded in university programmes either, their idea of creating physical schools for employees rather than putting them through mere *onboarding* or traditional corporate training programmes, was born out of a need to find a better way of folding training into education.

Universities can imprint their own cultures, values and methods onto their students, but they cannot imprint Google's culture, or Microsoft's values, or Apple's methods onto them without Google's, Microsoft's and Apple's involvement. This is the fundamental friction point along the education-to-training-to-job pipeline: as organizations come to realize the importance of culture, values and methods to their own continued success, the absence of those three dimensions in their new hires becomes a liability for hires, hiring organizations, universities and professional schools.

By partnering with major employers, and particular tech-sector employers, universities and professional schools will find themselves better able to develop the specialized workforce that these major employers need to build and drive towards their future. It isn't a stretch to imagine that research partnerships between technology companies and universities (in domains like artificial intelligence, engineering, robotics and so on) could morph into more structured and deliberate career preparation tracks, with companies like IBM, Microsoft, Google, and perhaps even Amazon and Apple, beginning to pursue the development of more formal university programmes focused on these fields in the next decade.

10. Adapting traditional educational institutions to a new world of human–machine partnerships

Do you teach a surgeon who will be operating on patients with robotic tools and AI-driven assistants differently from a surgeon who will operate with 20th-century tools?

The answer, obviously, is yes.

When thinking about the impact that human–machine partnerships will have on the way we train future professionals and on the practical skills we teach them, we quickly come to the same logical conclusion: universities and professional schools will have to invest in AR and VR technologies, AI capabilities, sophisticated cloud, fog and edge solutions, IoT solutions, robotics, virtual design tools, enterprise-class business analytics and decision-making tools.

They will have to teach workers of the future how to build, structure, train and manage teams of AIs, bots and digital assistants. They will also have to teach business leaders how to build and manage technology-driven organizations. Here, too, we see an opportunity for university programmes and professional schools to partner with technology vendors to deliver the type of training that real-world workers will need practical experience with, not just theoretical knowledge. Companies like SAP, Cisco, IBM, Alphabet, Microsoft, Amazon, Dassault Systèmes, Salesforce and others have an opportunity to partner with these institutions to help future workers and leaders in their respective fields become proficient in the use of their products. It's just that basic proficiency in Excel and PowerPoint will be taught alongside basic proficiency in multibot management, mixed-reality collaboration and ethical AI bias resolution. Universities and professional schools that want to remain competitive will have to develop these new courses and curricula sooner rather than later, and those will be best developed with the help of an as diverse as possible ecosystem of technology partners.

To do the job properly, universities and professional schools will also have to teach future workers how to transition from the old two-dimensional *tool/user* mindset that characterized most human–machine partnerships in the past to the more symbiotic human–machine partnership mindset that will define our daily work alongside machines. Secondly, they will have to keep up with the pace of change outside of academia. This means that universities will have to update their courses, technologies, methods and student evaluation criteria to match the needs of employers at a much higher velocity than they have traditionally been accustomed to. This acceleration in the pace of change may prove especially challenging for academic institutions that have, for most of their history, prided themselves on changing very little, and very slowly at that. As with all other industries, however, the ability (or inability) to adapt to change quickly and to be agile will have a direct impact on academic institutions' value, relevance and survival in an AI-driven world.

11. The case for liberal arts in a world of AI and technologists

For decades, the joke about the value of a liberal arts education has essentially been this:

> The engineering major asks, 'How does it work?'
> The accounting major asks, 'How much does it cost?'
> The liberal arts major asks, 'Would you like fries with that?'

In the real world, however, most liberal arts majors don't really end up working in fast-food restaurants. A 2014 study by the Association of American Colleges and Universities (AACU) revealed that by age 56–60 (peak earning years), liberal arts majors see their salaries peak near $66,000 on average, or some $2,000 higher than counterparts with professional degrees.[2]

While liberal arts majors tend to earn less than some of their STEM counterparts (upwards of $80,000 per year on average with science and maths degrees, and nearer to $100,000 on average with engineering degrees), these numbers don't account for liberal arts majors who go on to pursue graduate and post-graduate degrees, particularly in the legal profession, and increasingly, in technology fields. Jack Ma, founder of Alibaba, is a liberal arts major. So are e-commerce pioneer and Overstock CEO Patrick Byrne, FedEx founder and CEO Fred Smith, Disney CEO Bob Iger, Slack's Stewart Butterfield, YouTube's Susan Wojcicki, Airbnb's Brian Chesky and Facebook's Sheryl Sandberg, to name only a few. There has always been a place in a world of engineers and technologists for liberal arts majors, and that will not change as we move towards a human–machine partnership-driven economy.

One reason for this is that liberal arts majors can think more broadly about problems that may elude their STEM counterparts (like the unintended consequences of a new technology or product feature), think creatively about design, and empathize with a wide range of user needs and experiences. The gorgeous curves, materials and ergonomics of our favourite digital devices today weren't just the result of engineering. Product design is a creative process that requires soft skills, intuition, cultural awareness. In a technology-driven world in which user experiences are everything (we live, after all, in the

Liberal arts majors can think more broadly about problems that may elude their STEM counterparts.

age of experience), product and user experience (UX) designers with liberal arts backgrounds can make a profound difference in a company's success, and subsequently, its future.

They can also help smooth the edge off the often abrasive 'tech-bro' culture that is still all too common across the tech industry, and are uniquely equipped to help technologists develop intuitive, benevolent, ethical, human-like AIs who want to serve and assist their human users. The infinite nuances, subtleties and layers of cultural understanding that must be taught to AIs are not engineering or mathematical problems – at least not initially. Helping machines be more human, interact better with humans, partner better with humans, and help humans make better decisions will require liberal arts majors to be given a seat at the table right alongside their STEM and business school counterparts.

12. Training-on-demand and the imperatives of continuous training

It would be easy for the most cynical to deem the act of sitting in a classroom, at a physical university, as a matriculated student as 'old school'. Education is all online nowadays, isn't it? Why bother with physical classrooms when you can just learn from home, or at your desk, or on the train? But we aren't cynics, so we will refrain from taking sides in the never-ending *old vs new* debate. What we will say though, is that the traditional model of attending school and sticking to a rigorous class and examination schedule, is fortunately no longer the *only* option open to dedicated and ambitious students.

So here we are, one foot squarely in the regimented world of classrooms and lecture halls, and the other in a world of connected laptops, smartphones, tablets, AR goggles and VR headsets, as portable vehicles of anytime-learning. And if you are like us, you probably don't have time to take a sabbatical, list your home on Airbnb, and go audit classes halfway across the country (or around the world, for that matter). As wonderful as that plan may sound, most of us have responsibilities to take care of, careers to manage, families to spend time with, bills to pay, and daily lives we can't just put on pause whenever the time comes to learn a new skill or earn a new certificate of some kind.

Before we say anything else about this topic, it is incumbent upon us to remind everyone that not all universities are accredited, not all teachers are qualified to teach, and not all educational or training programmes are worth the price of admission. Before registering for any class, programme or certification track, do your research. Always make absolutely certain that you aren't being swindled by unscrupulous purveyors of educational snake oil. Learn the difference between universities and 'universities', teachers and 'teachers', and certifications and 'certifications'.

Assuming that you have a pretty good handle on which online and distance programmes are legitimate and which are not, the brave new world of distance education is now your oyster. All you really need to learn a new skill is an adequate interface, a decent Internet connection, a valid payment method and a few blocks of time in your schedule. Interested in data visualization modelling? There are online courses for that. Interested in dashboard design and management? There are online classes for that too. Do you need to start learning how to code, or how to work with mobile collaboration tools, or how to build AI-powered tools for your team? Check, check and check. If the popular saying a few years ago was 'there's an app for that', the new version of it is 'there's an online course for that'.

If it wasn't already obvious, here is why we bring this up: whether you are still in school or already an experienced professional, you will eventually have to update your skills and acquire new ones. And with the changes currently on the way, to say nothing of the pace of those changes, continuous training is going to become even more of a career imperative than it already was. You will be required to learn new skills, adapt to new tools, change the way you do things so regularly that online training will soon start to feel like it is part of your job, because in fact, it will be.

Just like human–machine partnerships, continuous training has to become a mentality before it can form into a habit. You have to understand why it matters and how. You have to be able to articulate its value in concrete, material terms, not just in the abstract. You have to not only understand but embrace the fact that in continuous training lies the key to adaptation, which in turn holds the key to your value to employers, partners or investors. The binary equations that determine your value are:

- Are you relevant or not?
- Do you know how to do [insert skill here] or not?
- Are you better at [insert skill here] than the simplest alternative?
- Are you more cost-effective than the simplest alternative?

That's it.

Having the new hot skill (or the old essential one needed in whatever relevant instance) will inform whether the answer to at least three out of these four questions is yes or no. If you care about your professional survival, you will work to make sure that the answer is always yes. And if professional survival isn't enough, and you prefer a more proactive approach to developing professional opportunities, you will also work to make sure that the answer is always yes. In either case, making sure that your skillset is adequate and up to date is as imperative as everything else your job asks of you. And what your job will soon ask of you will involve knowing how to build and manage virtual teams to boost your productivity, and automate tasks that can be properly automated.

As AI solutions open new doors for workers and leaders across pretty much every industry across the globe, your ability to learn, on the fly, how to leverage these new solutions to not only remain relevant but boost productivity, improve outcomes and positively transform your workplace, is going to become the closest thing to a superpower that you will ever experience professionally. Leveraging on-demand continuous training must become a career imperative for everyone hoping to remain relevant and competitive in an AI-driven economy.

CHAPTER SEVEN

How consumers should prepare for the next age of human– machine partnerships

How human–machine partnerships will impact our daily lives

It is impossible to talk about the impact that technology will continue to have on the daily lives of consumers without acknowledging that individuals' professional and private lives are becoming increasingly intertwined.

This has come about not only through changes in workplace expectations and work–life boundaries, but by smartphones, tablets and laptops, combined with ubiquitous Internet connectivity and the proliferation of mobile productivity apps (from traditional e-mail to agile collaboration software).

While countries like France have taken steps to re-establish some of these boundaries (French law now protects employees from having to respond to work e-mails during their off hours), the majority of the world has thus far failed to adequately address this friction point and we expect this trend to continue at least into the next decade.[1]

Despite the absence of clear demarcations between work-related human–machine partnerships and non-work human–machine partnerships, we will attempt to focus this chapter on the latter: how should consumers prepare for the next age of human–machine partnerships?

Before jumping into where these partnerships are going, let us take a moment to highlight some of the ways disruptive digital technologies like AI and smart automation are already changing the way consumers manage their affairs.

From search engines to recommendation engines

A good place to start would be to look at the way consumers now access and consume information. Over the course of the last two decades, newspapers and magazines have gone digital. According to a 2017 Pew Research study, 67 per cent of Americans now get their news from social media sources rather than from traditional news outlets, and 45 per cent get their news from Facebook.[2]

Algorithms now guide the way information is shared, accessed, recommended and managed.

In addition, search engines like Google and Bing now help consumers search for news items, relevant content and answers to their questions, and this changes the way that consumers interact with and consume information. For better or for worse, algorithms now guide the way information is shared, accessed, recommended and managed by billions of consumers around the world. The newspaper stand, the television set and the radio aren't the go-to information sources that they once were.

It would be easy to overlook the fact that search-focused algorithms are one of the most widespread and transformative human–machine partnerships already transforming the lives of consumers. Whether they are searching for news, product reviews, random bits of historical or literary knowledge, public transit schedules, medical advice, tax planning insights or holiday getaway packages, consumers around the world already turn to machines for help over 40,000 times per second and 1.2 trillion times per year.[3]

We begin with so-called 'search engines' because they are a mature, familiar human–machine partnership we all use daily. What consumers need to realize, however, is that because search engines are really *recommendation* engines, they can be leveraged to influence every aspect of our lives, from what we purchase to what we believe. Our language may need to change in order to reflect this shift in the balance of power between consumers and the technology platforms that help shape our opinions and guide our behaviours. 'Recommendation engines' remind us of what these tools actually do (as opposed to what consumers do on them).

In a best-case scenario, a recommendation algorithm will work in a Big Butler capacity to offer the best possible recommendations for its user, based on the user's needs. But in a less than perfect scenario, a compromised or less user-centric search engine may choose instead to make recommendations based on an advertiser's best interest, alter the order in which recommendations will appear or block certain types of recommendations altogether, without the user's knowledge.

As an example, Google was notably fined $2.7 billion by the European Commission in 2017 for allegedly favouring its own comparison shopping results.[4] While instances in which technology and media platforms that engage in self-interested manipulation of recommendations may not deserve to be thrown into the Big Brother bucket, these types of behaviours are antithetical to the user-centric 'Big Butler' *modus operandi* that consumers may assume whenever they opt to use recommendation engines.

As consumers have become dependent on this particular type of human–machine partnership, the extent to which behind-the-curtain algorithm manipulations of popular recommendations can be used by entities (companies, groups and governments alike) to shape public opinion, steer consumers towards certain products and away from others, and spread misinformation, should concern us all and demand closer scrutiny.

One could argue that platforms like Facebook, Twitter and YouTube, by leveraging algorithms to recommend content and ads to specific users, walk a very fine line between providing users with an optimally customized user-centric experience, and exploiting human weaknesses to influence opinions, behaviours and actions. Consider how easily specific demographics can be targeted by publishers of fake news and misinformation campaigns. Also consider how easily algorithms can be gamed to provide lift for certain types of content. And don't forget how easily these platforms can be used to disseminate fraudulent content through viral-like sharing by legitimate users, fake accounts and bots.

Whether a technology platform's parent company is complicit in the activity, or negligent, unaware or unable to stop it, is irrelevant. Consumers need to realize that the responsibility to determine if a human–machine partnership they opt into is toxic or harmful falls entirely on them. Even if regulatory bodies impose the application of warning labels and disclaimers on these tools, consumers must be vigilant, aware and proactive enough to protect themselves from the weaponization of recommendation engines, no matter where or how they are used.

Why trust is the next killer app

And this brings us to the topic of trust. All partnerships are built on a foundation of trust. No partnership that isn't can last. This means that if we are to successfully drive the adoption and ubiquitous use of consumer-centric human–machine partnerships, *trust* must be at the heart of every platform, technology and use case that will constitute a human–machine partnership in the future.

We must be able to *trust* that our self-driving cars will not crash into walls. We must be able to *trust* that our smart homes will not be used to spy on us or invade our privacy. We must be able to *trust* that our robot caretakers will not accidentally administer the wrong medication. We must be able to *trust* that our AI assistants will not share our financial, medical and personal information with unauthorized parties. We must be able to *trust* that algorithms that analyse our online and offline behaviours will not be used against us by hostile third parties.

Trust must be at the heart of every consumer-facing platform, app and technology for it to reach its full potential. Companies that understand this will thrive.

Where consumer-facing human–machine partnerships go from here: welcome to the age of 'AI Inside'

Everyone reading this book will no doubt be familiar with Intel's *Intel Inside* slogan, marking devices equipped with Intel chips. It was a clever slogan, an effective campaign and a good spring-board for this next segment of our discussion. As artificial intelligence begins to work its way into the fabric of our every-day lives, we may soon begin to see more and more objects we interface with become imbued with some form of AI-related functionality.

Enter the digital assistant. Whether your assistant of choice is Alexa, Siri, Cortana, Google Assistant or any other, digital assis-tants appear to be the next interface. When you hear journalists and analysts talk about *voice* being the next interface (replacing *touch*), that is what they mean. Instead of typing a search query, using your favourite connected device's screen or keyboard, you can simply speak it. Through a combination of edge and cloud computing, software can process and analyse your spoken commands, perform the query and respond both onscreen and through a voice interface.

Over 40 per cent of adults already used voice interfaces and digital assistants on a daily basis in 2016 to search for recipes, play music, schedule meetings, make hands-free phone calls, turn on their TV, obtain directions in their car, and make online purchases.[5] The convenience, ease, and even the charming novelty of interacting in a human way with machines, are contributing to a rapid adoption of voice-interface technologies, at the heart of which sit AI-powered digital assistants.

From a technology standpoint, not just a matter of human preference, the digital assistant code has been cracked, and there is no going back. Artificial intelligence doesn't necessarily require an Internet connection: voice, face and gesture recognition capabilities, natural language processing, intelligent functionality and even security are now built right into the chips that power smart devices. While AI can and often does also live in the cloud, its functional core now lives on the edge of digital networks, inside the interfacing hardware. Smart devices all have some degree of built-in AI functionality that will continue to improve and grow in the coming decades.

The same can be said of cloud-based consumer-facing applications, from the recommendation engines we discussed earlier to advanced CRM (customer relationship management) systems brands use to drive loyalty, purchases and recommendations among their customers. Artificial intelligence can identify opportunities for companies to optimize their signal-to-noise ratio by engaging their customers with the right offers at the right time. Artificial intelligence can also identify which customers may be losing interest and target them with special offers or rewards before they are too far gone. Artificial intelligence can take on the hybrid Big Butler/Big Mother role of suggesting certain products and services, and provide advice, unprompted, when the occasion presents itself.

The opportunities to optimize consumer-friendly transaction-based experiences are limitless when intelligent computers are assigned a dual business development and customer service role simultaneously. Where competing departments like sales, marketing and customer service were once disjointed and unable to operate together in real time and at scale, AI-powered software can, and for a fraction of the cost of attempting to make humans handle it.

Even non-transactional interactions with consumers can be optimized by AI-powered CRM algorithms. Once an airline knows that you are 48 hours away from a trip, an AI may decide to send you a text with friendly packing and travel tips. 24 hours away from departure, an AI may send you reminders about what documents to bring with you, and links to useful information about your departure airport and terminal. While you are in transit, an AI may send you your next gate number and boarding information. The same kind of natural, intuitive, unprompted digital assistant functionality can be used to help consumers make the best of their current trip to the grocery store, or motivate them during a workout, or safely discover an unfamiliar part of the world.

Always having access to an intuitive, benevolent and resourceful digital assistant, whether through a personal device or a public interface, is at the heart of the 'AI Inside' revolution that will power the next phase of consumer-facing human–machine partnerships.

Google's Duplex project, dubbed 'the smartest chatbot ever' by *Digital Trends* and introduced to the world in the spring of 2016, has an ambitious goal: to transform today's rudimentary AIs (capable of basic natural language analysis but still plagued by limited human-like functionality) into a life-like AI, presumably capable of beating a Turing test.[6] Among Duplex's specific objectives: create an AI that sounds life-like, that can analyse a user's mood and state of mind in real time, that can remember previous conversations in order to reference them again as needed, and remember where a previous conversation ended so it can pick it up where it left off at a later time, just like a human being can.

This is where AI is going next: not sci-fi inspired mildly robotic-sounding assistants, but entirely human-sounding AIs with the ability to perfectly mimic human speech patterns, tone, mood, personalities and behaviours. Not only that, but this next generation of AIs will also have the ability to mimic subtle human emotions and therefore communicate empathy, sympathy, humour and care to users when they most need it.

How will smart automation and AI help drive smart home automation?

We begin this section discussing home automation because it is one of the most obvious consumer-facing categories of human–machine partnerships already observable today. The premise is simple – a smart home promises to extend the functionality of a digital assistant to the entire home.

To understand just how fundamental the changes brought on by the mass adoption of smart home technologies will be, consider two of the most common and frequently used interfaces in any modern dwelling: the door key, and the light switch. A century from now, neither might exist any more.

Keys have already begun to disappear from the automotive experience. Keyless entry and keyless ignition systems have all but eliminated the need for physical keys, relegating them to emergency backup roles when systems fail and tools must be used to get out of a jam. When it comes to cars, keys have already begun to be seen as remnants of a bygone analogue era. Homes are the next place this will happen. Why carry keys when you can unlock your door at the push of a button or with a simple voice command? Why carry a key or a set of keys when your face and your voice are all you need to lock and unlock your front door? For better or for worse, electronic locks will replace analogue locks, and eliminate the need for consumers to carry any keys at all.

A similar fate awaits light switches. Why walk to a light switch and flick the lights on or off with your hand when you can make the lights come on with a voice command? Why stop there? The same voice interface that can turn the lights on and off without having to get up and walk to a wall switch can also dim or brighten the lights, adjust their hue and set them to various energy-saving modes.

Keys and wall switches: our great grandchildren may only ever see them in photos and museums. Universal points of reference like keys and switches are never trivial, and neither is their disappearance. They mark a definitive evolution from analogue homes to digital homes, and beyond that, from 'dumb' electrified homes to 'thinking' intelligent homes.

It would be easy to mistake the age of smart homes as merely being about AI-powered gadget proliferation inside the home, but we believe that the coming change will be more fundamental than that: our homes won't just be dwellings any more. Our homes will soon begin to play an *active* part in taking care of us, in cooking our food, in stocking our pantries, in keeping us safe, in helping us be physically and mentally healthy, in keeping us informed and engaged with the outside world, and at no time in human history has that been the case. Smart home technology promises to make dwellings active partners in people's daily lives.

Consider scenarios in which a smart home is tasked with monitoring the vitals and physical well-being of an individual, detecting an emergency in the home like an electrical fire or gas leak, reporting a crime in real time or monitoring the occupants' nutrition and well-being. How many medical emergencies will be reported and lives saved? How many disasters will be averted? How many crimes will be prevented, or previously unsolvable cases solved? How many individuals' lives will be enriched physically and mentally? And in all these examples, to what extent will the smart home not only passively monitor, alert and report, but also prevent, prepare and solve?

A smart home might be able to automatically detect and immediately report child abuse, spousal abuse, break-ins, assaults and even murders, for instance. Data collected by a smart home's appliances may be able to detect a nutritional deficiency or diagnose a yet-undetected medical condition the way smart beds can already help identify and solve sleeping disorders. Smart appliances and utility management hubs can help optimize water and power consumption, monitor environmental conditions, and not only detect but filter out environmental pollutants and contaminants like moulds, smog, smoke, allergens, toxic aerosols. A smart home can help make sure that children are doing their homework, that parental controls on every device in the home are active, that they aren't putting themselves in danger while their parents are away.

Smart homes aren't just fancy gadget ecosystems. They could play a critical role in prolonging the lives of the more physically and psychologically vulnerable among us by ensuring, for instance, that people living with dementia or Alzheimer's take the right medication at the right time, that stoves aren't inadvertently left on, that no electrical devices plugged into a wall are near pooling water, that doors and windows are locked when they should be, and that the right people are notified if the patient becomes disoriented, confused, or finds him- or herself in distress.

Smart homes can similarly help people who suffer from loneliness and depression by engaging with them, facilitating social interactions, and helping them focus on positive rather than negative thoughts. Although no substitute for treatment or human contact, a smart home's AI can be a gardening coach, a cooking teacher, a pet whisperer, a maths tutor, a personal reader, a therapist, a fitness instructor, a medical advisor, even a shoulder to cry on if need be, and all of these roles can make a difference in millions of lives. It isn't inconceivable that smart homes may not only succeed in combating loneliness but some day in helping prevent suicides as well.

Smart homes are not about adding voice and superficial AI functionality to various appliances for novelty's sake. The value of smart homes, looking beyond the near horizon of the next few years, is far more life-changing than what a trip to your local electronics store might currently suggest. Smart lighting and smart speakers are merely the superficial edges of what will become guardian homes, companion homes and caretaker homes in the coming age of AI-powered human–home partnerships.

How will smart automation and AI impact transportation and infrastructure?

We could easily devote an entire book to the impact AI and smart automation are likely to have on transportation, but since we only have a few pages to spare, let us focus on the most critical aspects of this impending revolution: autonomous passenger vehicles, autonomous commercial vehicles and autonomous public transportation infrastructure.

Before we can really talk about specific use cases, we must address the technological fabric that will eventually make autonomous vehicles work in the real world, and particularly in busy and often cramped urban environments. On the one hand, vehicles must come equipped with a certain degree of built-in autonomy powered by sensors, computer vision and a sophisticated onboard AI, but that isn't enough. For an autonomous vehicle to be able to safely interact with its environment, it must also rely on three additional systems that it must be able to manage and integrate into its navigation and autopilot system simultaneously. These systems are usually referred to as V2V, V2P and V2I. The V, P and I correspond to vehicle, pedestrian and infrastructure, respectively.

Most smart and semi-autonomous vehicles today already come equipped with V2V systems that allow them to identify other vehicles, sense their size, speed and direction of travel (as applicable), and interpret their behaviour (accelerating, turning, drifting or braking, for instance). These V2V systems can range from rudimentary sensor-powered features that notify a driver of the presence of a car in their 'blind spot' to sophisticated driver-assist and crash-avoidance systems that compensate for a driver's delayed reaction time in an emergency by automatically initiating a safety manoeuvre and guiding the driver's behaviour through the emergency. With the exception of self-parking capabilities, which are already becoming quite reliable, V2V systems are currently the most advanced of the three, with V2P (vehicle to pedestrian) and V2I (vehicle to infrastructure) capabilities still lagging behind.

Despite rapid advances in computer vision, it is still difficult for today's semi-autonomous vehicles to reliably identify pedestrians from their surroundings in all weather and light conditions, let alone teach onboard autopilots to predict their behaviour. It is also difficult for semi-autonomous vehicles to interface with surrounding infrastructure as, to date, said infrastructure is not yet specifically geared towards optimizing autonomous vehicles performance or safety, particularly in dense urban environments.

Sadly, for all of the marketing and brand journalism done around the impending self-driving car revolution, most of us will likely not be driven to work or to the dentist's office by a self-driving car any time soon. Massive investments in transportation infrastructure, silicon, AI, edge compute, and even the 5G networks that will form the V2I connective fabric necessary for our cities to become autonomous-vehicle-friendly will be required to transition from where we are today to where we hope to be in the future. Technology is not the real problem. The scale of investment into new infrastructure is. Retrofitting our roads, streets and cities into spaces where pedestrians and autonomous vehicles can co-exist will be herculean in scope, and may take several decades to see itself fully realized.

The exact trajectory of the impact that vehicle autonomy will have on transportation is especially difficult to predict because it puts in question the need for consumers to own a car. Why? Because in a future in which cars can drive themselves, cars can also park themselves, pick up your dry-cleaning and deliver it to your house, and even drive around looking for other passengers to transport from Point A to Point B while you aren't using it. In a future populated by cars that drive themselves, and which are therefore imbued with exponentially more agency than they do today, the utility of a single car changes from that of an expensive and quickly depreciating personal transportation device that spends the majority of its time taking up space to that of a fluid, high-utility transportation robot with the potential to serve dozens if not hundreds of users per day.

The question becomes this: why leave your self-driving car sitting in a parking space all day while you work, when it could be earning money driving other people around, or making itself useful by running errands for you – like picking up your kids from school or swinging by the store to pick up tonight's dinner? And once you begin to think of your car as a utility transportation robot, which it now is, you have to start asking yourself if it makes sense to own your car by yourself or if it makes more sense to perhaps co-own it instead, or even to subscribe to a monthly fleet-access service that makes any one of hundreds of vehicles instantly accessible to you, and charges you based on your individual vehicle usage? In other words, as cars become fully autonomous, and their utility increases as described, does the traditional model of car ownership that we have all known thus far potentially evolve as well? Do self-driving cars become so commoditized that we begin to treat them more as self-driving taxis than personal possessions, particularly in urban environments?

The implications are staggering, as such a scenario would force civil engineers, city planners and public transportation utilities to completely rethink their infrastructure plans. More utility per vehicle could translate into more traffic throughout the day but perhaps less congestion during formerly peak congestion hours. More utility per vehicle could also mean that more charging stations would have to be installed throughout a city to keep those fleets of vehicles running all day long. It also means that far less space would be required for parking, as fewer vehicles would experience downtime during the day. In a single city, tens of thousands of parking spaces may no longer be needed, freeing up space for wider sidewalks, green spaces and new construction. Fleets of self-driving cars could eliminate the need for subways, buses and trams in certain parts of the city, as they would become a substitute form of public transportation.

Even in the suburbs, a shift from traditional car ownership to a commoditized access to vehicle-on-demand services means that homes may no longer require a garage at all, allowing homeowners to either make more effective use of their homes' square footage or build smaller-footprint homes.

The benefits of having autonomous vehicles on the road long before we reach that stage could also be potentially life-changing for millions of motorists, cyclists and pedestrians each year. As cars gain the ability to take their drunk owners home when they are not fit to drive, it is likely that drunk-driving accidents may one day become a thing of the past. Smart vehicles should also eventually help neutralize dangerous human-driver behaviours like distracted driving, aggressive driving, driving with inadequate corrective eyewear, and driving too fast for conditions, turning our streets and roadways into far safer environments than they have ever been.

According to the *Global Status Report on Road Safety 2018*, over a million people die in traffic-related accidents around the world each year, road traffic injuries are among the leading causes of death for children and young adults (aged 5–29), and a leading cause of death for people of all ages.[7] In our view, the faster we are able to effectuate a safe transition from semi-autonomous vehicle use to fully-autonomous vehicle use at scale, the faster we can begin solving this problem.

How will smart automation and AI transform the way we shop?

Our objective here isn't to put our futurist hats on and prognosticate all the fun ways that shopping might be transformed by smart automation and AI. What we want to do instead is look at current retail behaviour trajectories, understand what existing pain points for retailers and shoppers might be ironed out by better human–machine partnerships, and identify some of the most significant changes that technology vendors are likely to inject into tomorrow's shopping ecosystem.

What we already see today:

- augmented reality used by retailers to help consumers shop for furniture, by allowing them to place virtual products, in three-dimensional space, in the spaces where they are intended to go;
- augmented reality used by retailers to help consumers shop for eyeglasses, clothes, fashion accessories and new hair styles;
- augmented reality used by retailers to enhance the in-store shopping experience for customers – with virtual offers, virtual ingredients lists on food items, store-mapping, augmented mirrors and in-store gamification;
- digital assistants being used as digital shopping assistants;
- AI-generated shopping lists and shopping recommendations;
- real-time, location-based, AI-driven ads targeting likely customers with optimized special offers;
- cross-platform ads driven by consumers' recent online searches;
- a steady annual increase in e-commerce, with online sales likely to exceed 12 per cent of total US retail sales by 2020;
- the rise of home deliveries;
- frictionless bricks-and-mortar shopping (virtualized checkouts).

Here is how we expect these key trend lines to evolve over the next 10–15 years: more of the same but better. Better technology integration. Better omnichannel experiences (in which online shopping, bricks-and-mortar shopping, digital touchpoints, and bricks-and-mortar touchpoints are all seamlessly intertwined). More shopping and delivery options for consumers. More AI-driven shopping experiences. More shopping automation.

The most valuable commodity in retail isn't space or inventory. It's time. On the retailer end, that translates into man-hours to pick, pack, ship, receive, stock, restock, checkout, maintain, clean and so on. On the consumer end, that translates into going to the store, shopping at the store, checking out, going home and putting the new items away. Human–machine partnerships tend to be, at their core, about improving efficiency and reducing the amount of work required to complete a task. From farming to filing, smart automation is about saving time to allow humans to focus on more important or valuable tasks.

Smart automation is about saving time to allow humans to focus on more valuable tasks.

Every study we have looked at comes to the same conclusion: the most repetitive, least fulfiling tasks and jobs are always the first to be automated. There is no reason why this logic will not be applied here as well. What problems are retailers and shoppers trying to solve? Spend less time on every task. What can be automated? Just about every task neither particularly enjoys spending a millisecond on that they don't absolutely have to. Looking at the future of retail through a human–machine partnership lens, what we see is primarily a universe of opportunity whose main goal will be to gain cost and time efficiencies by automating as much of the shopping process as possible.

With regard to bricks-and-mortar retail, we foresee the near end of checkout lines, and of physical checkouts altogether. Amazon Go's virtual checkout model, in which the checkout happens automatically, without requiring a shopper to scan or weigh products before paying, will be emulated by major retailers like Walmart in the United States, and will reset consumer expectations with regard to a cluster of universal checkout friction points. No one wants to wait in line, no one enjoys having to unpack products then repack them, and even payment transactions at a terminal can be tedious. Eliminating these pain points and time constraints from the retail experience by completely automating the checkout process and allowing customers to simply pick the items they came to purchase and walk out of the store will enjoy mass adoption, particularly in areas where cashless payments have become the norm.

We also expect a cluster of technologies including AI, social platforms, data-mining platforms, facial recognition, beacons, digital ID and the IoT to deliver real-time, personalized omnichannel experiences for customers. Whether these technologies will be opt-in or opt-out by default for consumers remains to be seen (and will depend on individual countries' stances with regard to privacy and consumer protections), but retailers developing the ability to track individual customers' behaviours online *and* in their physical stores is already well underway. The ability to track, analyse and predict individual behaviours in real time, and at scale, will shape the future of retail marketing and omnichannel experiences. Consumers should expect more time-relevant, custom-tailored offers, experiences and rewards from retailers to become the norm in the coming decade.

We also anticipate seeing large retailers rethink their retail space footprint as online orders, delivery requests and autonomous delivery vehicles begin to outpace physical in-store visits by customers. We expect to see existing retail spaces converted, at least in part, into online order-fulfilment centres where orders, once received digitally, can be picked, packed and made ready for pickup or delivery. At first, these fulfilment centres will be staffed by human workers, but in the long term, the process will become mostly automated, with machines handling the order-fulfilment process. Shoppers will have the option to either pick up their orders themselves or arrange for them to be delivered. These deliveries will initially be handled by human drivers in traditional delivery vehicles, but as driverless service vehicles increasingly take over the task, especially in densely populated areas (where delivery robots can achieve the greatest efficiency and provide the highest rate of return) deliveries will increasingly become automated as well.

We also anticipate smart appliances and smart home technologies to allow consumers to automate at least some of their shopping process. In its most basic form, this will manifest itself as AI-generated shopping lists based on user needs and preferences. A smart refrigerator, capable of sensing that a user is running out of eggs or milk, will have the capacity to recommend a milk and egg purchase, and generate an up-to-date shopping list. Other smart appliances and technologies throughout the home will also be able to notify a user that he or she is running out of cleaning supplies, canned goods, laundry soap, razor blades, cat food and whatever else needs to be restocked. At the more proactive end of the spectrum, the smart home or digital assistant managing the smart home will have been given the autonomy to place restocking orders as needed, without requiring human intervention. This is an example of Big Butler in action.

With regard to augmented reality and virtual reality technologies embedding themselves into the retail ecosystem, we believe that any technology that can create remarkable brand experiences, facilitate the selection of the right products, save customers time, save retailers money and improve the frequency, reach and yield of both brand interactions and purchases, will find rich and friendly soil in which to grow.

Ultimately, consumers themselves, as the users of AR and VR technologies, will decide how effective or useful that particular application of digital technology will be to their shopping experience. We anticipate AR to enjoy a far greater rate of adoption than VR, especially as AR glasses become smaller, lighter, cheaper and more fashionable than they are today. If AR headset makers can shift even 30 per cent of mobile users' screen time from their handheld mobile device to AR glasses, AR will become a factor in bricks-and-mortar retail experiences. If they cannot, AR's potential importance to retail may never be fully realized.

As we mentioned already, recommendation engines are also likely to play a significant role in driving consumer behaviours, both online and offline, and we expect digital influence, driven by layers of cloud and edge machine learning and AI-powered algorithms, to be a powerful force in helping streamline consumer choices. One specific way that recommendation engine technology could create a useful human–machine partnership is if consumers are given the ability to optimize the recommendation engines they use to filter out advertising noise in favour of advertising signal. That is, essentially act as a smart ad blocker that intuitively filters out any ad or marketing offer that a consumer is unlikely to be interested in, and prioritize ads and marketing offer that are most likely to be useful to that consumer. The ability to leverage a recommendation engine as gatekeeper as opposed to an instrument of manipulation and influence rests entirely on that recommendation engine's willingness to allow a user to set its rules and preferences as opposed to the platform imposing them on a user. Keep an eye out for customizable, opt-in recommendation engines. The more Big Butler a recommendation engine is, the more likely it is to drive a healthy and useful human–machine partnership.

How will smart automation and AI shape the future of healthcare and homecare?

We have already addressed some of the ways that smart homes will help the care and well-being of individuals, but we mostly discussed the role that digital assistants and passive smart home technologies play in that endeavour. Let us now focus on some of the more active, and dare we call them 'mechanical', smart automation technologies that we believe will transform home-care and healthcare in the coming two decades.

Starting with homecare then, let's begin with the intersection of sensor technology, AI and telemedicine. First, sensors tasked with monitoring health-related data can help observe a patient's health around the clock with little to no intervention from a human nurse or healthcare professional. Secondly, these data streams can be fed to apps, simultaneously on the edge of a network and in the cloud, that can monitor, analyse and react to them in real time. IoT devices can then perform any number of tasks, from notifying the patient of a problem and recommend-ing a course of action to administering medicine and alerting specialized healthcare responders. A patient might be prompted by an AI to walk around the house for a few minutes, drink a glass of water, sit down for a few moments to de-stress, and to answer questions that will determine whether they are fully alert or suffering from a stroke or temporarily confused.

Advances in telemedicine also make it increasingly possible for patients to interact directly with medical professionals with-out having to leave their homes. This is not only convenient for homebound patients and medical professionals themselves; it is also convenient for busy individuals who may require light check-ups or short discussions with a medical professional.

A patient can in a few minutes have a physician to discuss symptoms, the effectiveness of a treatment, and so on, from the comfort of their office or home. The value of that type of approach to health management should be self-explanatory. This model, aided by the proliferation of faster and more advanced 4G and 5G networks, should become far more main-stream than it is today over the course of the next decade.

One area of particular interest to us within the framework of human–machine partnership is the possibility that robots and AIs may begin to play a far more significant role in healthcare.

At the most extreme high end of the healthcare robotics spectrum are surgery robots, which could some day replace human surgeons in a variety of surgical interventions and other medical tasks.

At the low end of that spectrum are patient management AIs that can organize, manage and update medical records without human intervention, saving time, cutting operational costs for hospitals and insurance providers, reducing the risk of errors, and potentially establishing more complete medical records for patients from previously disconnected databases.

More sophisticated AIs may also be employed to search a patient's medical records for potential health risks and yet unflagged sensitivities to certain types of medication and identify likely areas of preventative care. DNA data, along with other health-related data contained in a patient's records, can be analysed by an AI to identify potential risks like cancer, heart disease, risk of stroke and even rare genetic defects, that traditional healthcare may not have detected early enough to prevent or treat in time.

The cloud, by adding scale to this type of deep learning application, can help expand it to millions of patients, improving the efficiency and focus of otherwise limited healthcare resources, reducing overall healthcare-related costs and increasing the likelihood of positive outcomes for large swathes of the population. The deployment of this model may initially vary from place to place, and is likely to be driven more by regional and national attitudes towards access to preventative healthcare technologies than by the availability of those technologies. Having said that, it is likely that, as all new technologies eventually become commoditized, AI-powered preventative health analysis will eventually become affordable to all, either through private or public service providers.

Bear in mind that we are not suggesting that AIs and robots will take the place of highly-skilled human healthcare professionals, but rather that they will enhance them. The same types of human–machine partnerships already discussed throughout this book apply to healthcare as well. For example, a physician, augmented by AIs, will be better equipped to diagnose a patient's possible health risk much better than they might have on their own. A surgical team, augmented by surgical robots, may be able to double the number of procedures it can perform in a day *and* significantly improve outcomes for patients. A nurse, augmented by AIs and medical robots, may be able to delegate otherwise tedious and repetitive tasks to machines and instead focus on more important and rewarding tasks. It is still imperative that skilled and experienced humans continue to make medical decisions for themselves and for patients, and that machines be used to advise and assist human professionals in their healthcare functions, not replace them outright.

We expect to see a partnership develop between human healthcare and homecare professionals in which one human nurse or caretaker, by partnering with an ecosystem of robots (perhaps a team of robots, perhaps a network of robots) will be able to manage a portfolio of patients around the clock.

Lastly, we expect that human–machine partnerships, particularly with regard to AI, deep learning and cognitive computing solutions, will help accelerate the pace of medical research. We have already observed how technology companies like Dassault Systèmes, which develops advanced 3D modelling (even at the molecular level) and virtualization tools, are partnering with medical researchers to help prevent and treat common medical conditions like heart anomalies and strokes.[8] In the same vein, we also already observe medical researchers partnering with intelligent computers to understand the link between certain DNA markers and health conditions.

This critical human–machine partnership will, in our view, revolutionize the field of medicine over the course of the next two decades, by augmenting our brightest minds with precisely the kind of computing, analysis and scale required to accelerate the search for cures and vaccines that would otherwise take generations to discover. Discovery is only half of the equation though: circling back to the role that advanced 3D modelling and virtualization can play in healthcare, virtualizing drug testing, genetic therapy, and new generations of cures and vaccines for common diseases will also help accelerate delivery timelines for these solutions.

What this means for patients, as consumers of healthcare solutions, is that the way we think of illness, medicine, patient care and health management is likely to radically change in the next decade. Patients will have access to a toolkit never before seen in human history and have the ability to better manage their own health and be alerted to potential problems much earlier than they used to.

Cloud-based analytics tools will also help patients identify genetic predispositions for certain types of illnesses, detect early onset symptoms and help AI-assisted physicians customize their treatment. Specialized AIs, smart environments and robots, will not only increase bandwidth for medical professionals, but serve as a far more effective medical emergency tripwire than the not-yet-automated medical emergency model in existence around the world today. Surgical robots will help reduce mishaps during surgeries and improve outcomes, but most importantly, they may help bring top-rate surgical capabilities usually reserved for top-tier metropolitan hospitals to small, out-of-the-way hospitals that struggle to attract top surgical talent. Homebound patients suffering from motor challenges, cognitive challenges, or even emotional challenges like loneliness and depression, will have the ability to turn to caretaker and companion robots to provide them with the kind of autonomy, security, emotional support and dignity they require to enjoy a quality of life.

The future of medicine is perhaps more dependent on human–machine partnerships than any other topic we have touched on in this book, and one of the areas about which we are most hopeful.

What will be the impact of smart automation and AI on our lifestyles and relationships?

We already mentioned how smart automation, from digital assistants, workforce augmentation and recommendation engines to autonomous vehicles, self-managing homes, and frictionless payments will free consumers from a wide range of menial, unrewarding and time-consuming tasks. The question now becomes: what will consumers do with all of that extra time? The simplest answer is: whatever they want.

For some, the extra time will become an opportunity to work longer hours, take on additional responsibilities or pursue new revenue opportunities. For others, it will become an opportunity to spend more time with loved ones, pursue a new certification or degree, pick up a hobby, read more, travel more, volunteer more, or perhaps invent the next big disruptive technology. For the optimist in all of us, more time means more opportunity, more freedom and an improved quality of life.

But for the pessimist in us, a world increasingly driven by smart automation also has downsides: top of mind is the very real risk that basic and critical human skillsets, once broadly relegated to smart automation, may be lost for ever. Skillsets that will matter when, for one reason or another, a failure in the technological fabric of society forces humans to have to become self-reliant again, whether for an hour or for the rest of their lives.

Once we become accustomed to machines doing everything for us, do we lose the ability to fix things when they break, to save a life in the midst of a medical emergency, to make the right split-second decision when catastrophe strikes? Do we lose the ability to discern fact from fiction or fake news from factual news reporting? Do we lose the ability to write or type or spell words properly? Do we lose the ability to make critical business or financial decisions? If the machine breaks – or rather *when* it does – will we still know how to be self-reliant enough to survive?

Another question we must ask ourselves, and which we deliberately keep bringing up because it is *that* important, is this: if we get so comfortable with machines increasingly guiding our every decision, from what to purchase and where to what to read or watch and when, do we not expose ourselves to machine-assisted manipulation and control? Could recommendation engines and life-like AIs be weaponized to turn us against each other, to steer public opinion in favour of questionable policies, to conceal fraudulent behaviours by hostile actors, to fraudulently vilify companies or dissidents, to marginalize certain groups, even to influence an otherwise independent judiciary? Can the technology we put our trust in ultimately be used to spy on us, to manipulate us and to control us? Can technology marketed to the public through Big Butler and Big Mother use cases be used to pursue Big Brother objectives? The answer is definitively yes.

Human–machine partnerships must be built on a firm foundation of trust.

It is therefore more imperative than ever that consumers remember that every smart automation tool that is not under their complete control cannot and should not be trusted. As with any successful partnership, human–machine partnerships must be built on a firm foundation of trust. Trust is a process of constant evaluation. The more dependent we become on smart automation technologies, the more conscious we must become of our own responsibility to ensure that these technologies will not be used against us, and the more responsible we must be for the way in which we use it to improve our own lives.

Here's the trap: the temptation in a world of smart automation and human–machine partnerships in which we increasingly delegate decisions and skills to digital assistants and machines is to also delegate our own agency. The irony here is that the very people who consciously fear that they will be replaced by machines tend to also fail to appreciate how easily they will naturally surrender their own autonomy, independence and self-reliance to machines in exchange for convenience.

The most effective way to avoid falling into that trap is to become mindful that 100 per cent of the time gained from smart automation efficiencies is an opportunity to develop and improve our own individual agency. If time is about opportunity, opportunity is about choices, and choices must always be our own. Even if an AI helps us decide between a movie or a football game, between a trip to Thailand or a trip to Egypt, between spending money or investing it, between taking a new job or staying where we are, the decision must always remain ours to make. In an age of AI-driven everything, holding on to our own agency becomes all the more paramount. Every single instance of smart automation and human–machine partnership is ultimately designed to give us *more* agency, not less. The moment we forget that is the moment we allow technology to control us instead of doing what we developed it to do: serve us.

> In an age of AI-driven everything, holding on to our own agency becomes all the more paramount.

This discussion is fundamental to any discussion about how smart automation and AI might impact our lifestyles and relationships, because both are entirely dependent on individual agency. Relying on AIs and smart automation to give us more time to spend on things we enjoy doing will make our everyday lives feel more rewarding. Relying on AIs and smart automation to achieve desired outcomes and improve performance will build our confidence in our own ability to achieve more than we already have, and to have a valuable impact on the world. Taking control of the parts of our lives that matter most to us by delegating the ones that matter least to machines is how we leverage human–machine partnerships to become more independent, not less.

The gift that human–machine partnerships bestows on our lifestyles and relationships is therefore *more* agency, not less. Those among us who realize this will reap the benefits of the human–machine partnerships that help shape their everyday lives. Those who fail to grasp this, and consequently fail to properly leverage human–machine partnerships to achieve *more* freedom, will likely find themselves wrestling with a daisy chain of opposite and adverse effects: less agency, less autonomy and less opportunity. Caution ahead.

How will smart automation and AI impact the way consumers think about life planning?

One underappreciated opportunity for consumers in an age of AI, smart automation, and human–machine partnership focuses on their ability to better plan for their future and navigate the intricacies and constant sea changes that affect their lives. By partnering with specialized deep learning machines, consumers will increasingly have more control over their educational trajectories, careers, finances, investments and retirement. Access to sophisticated predictive algorithms will improve their ability to anticipate and plan for market fluctuations, geopolitical shifts, changes in workforce trends, even shifting home values by neighbourhood.

Imagine being a homebuyer with access to a predictive analytics tool that can map the trajectory of home values in every neighbourhood in which you are currently considering an investment. Would that not be helpful? Imagine the same type of analytics tool being applied to how the college of your choice might score the 20 different high schools that your children might attend, 10 to 15 years from now, based on which home you decide to buy.

Now consider how you might invest your money differently if you know, early in life, thanks to sophisticated diagnostics tools, that you will likely require multiple heart surgeries before you reach retirement age. Consider how sophisticated financial advisor AIs (or human financial advisors augmented by intelligent analytics tools) will be able to better help you plan your career, life and finances to prepare for what is coming.

In the previous section, we spoke about agency. Having access to better data, better analytics and concrete solutions like these illustrates how human–machine partnerships can be leveraged to enjoy *more* agency, more control over one's own life, and more opportunities to prepare for the inevitable rough spots that might have otherwise derailed it. We expect that banks, insurance providers, real estate brokers and financial advisors will soon begin to make these tools centrepieces of their service offerings, but the real opportunity here may actually rest in the hands of individual customers looking to customize their own third-party analytics and life-planning toolkits in order to avoid being influenced by deliberate in-tool bias and less-than-neutral advice. Integration with popular AI assistants will most likely drive mass-market adoption for software providers of such tools.

The point being that much of the guesswork and instinct-based decisions that have always guided many of the public's most life-affecting decisions – from choosing a school and buying a home to accepting one job offer over another to effectively planning for retirement – will increasingly be replaced by mathematically-sound probability models and predictive analytics-based recommendation engines. Whether the shift from instinct to data analytics will ultimately prove as effective as one hopes remains to be seen, but the possibility that it may result in improved outcomes (more financial security, more career opportunities, improved quality of life, better health, etc) is certainly worth the attempt.

How should we protect our personal safety and privacy in the age of smart automation and AI?

For consumers, smart automation is a double-edged sword: on the one hand smart automation technologies can help cut through the tedium, clutter and time-suck that most people want off their plates. On the other, it exposes consumers to unprecedented vulnerabilities with regard to privacy, data security and personal freedoms.

We already know that mountains of consumer data are being collected by technology companies. This is the reality of the world we live in, and the price we pay for living in an increasingly technologically driven world. But unlike some of our colleagues, and a growing ecosystem of doomsday pundits, we do not believe that consumers have no choice but to surrender their privacy and expectations of basic data security in exchange for the benefits and conveniences of a digitally augmented society.

Transitions are always difficult and messy, and as we write this book, the world is in the midst of a significant transition from dumb automation and a rudimentary digital economy into an entirely new ecosystem of smart automation and a powerful, AI-driven digital economy. The challenges we currently face with regard to privacy, data security and IoT security are temporary growing pains. Technology development as we write this book is decentralized, uneven, unpredictable and at times chaotic. Legislation and regulations aiming to protect consumers from abuse struggle to keep up with the pace of technology innovation. More often than not, vulnerabilities are discovered and exploited by hackers faster than they can be patched up, and increasingly, AIs and bots are being deployed by hackers to both scale and accelerate their attacks on vulnerable systems in an attempt to overwhelm their defences. And here is where we begin to glimpse the solution to this problem: if machines can be leveraged by hackers and hostile actors to discover vulnerabilities in systems and networks, and attack them, machines can also be leveraged by system and network administrators to plug up vulnerabilities, detect attacks and deploy countermeasures against them.

As we enter the new millennium's third decade, the cybersecurity space is about to undergo as profound a change as the rest of the world. Instead of man vs machine, battles fought across that particular battlefield will be mostly machine vs machine, with

The cybersecurity space is about to undergo as profound a change as the rest of the world.

algorithms battling algorithms, viruses battling antiviruses, AIs battling AIs and advanced silicon capable of protecting itself from unwanted intrusions or attacks. In other words, privacy and data security concerns may, over the course of the next decade, become far less of a problem than it has been thus far.

In the meantime, here are some steps that consumers should begin to take to protect their data and their privacy:

- Demand that lawmakers and political leaders become technology-literate, and that they take technology-facing legislation seriously.
- Lobby for and support data security and privacy legislation (like GDPR).
- Voice privacy concerns to technology companies and demand that they provide users with tools to opt-in and opt-out of data collection programs at will, and that data collection programs be made entirely transparent for users.
- Support technology companies whose products are designed to protect their users' privacy and give them control over the data they agree to share and not share.
- For confidential communications, only use solutions with certified end-to-end encryption.
- Look for IoT devices with built-in security at the chip level (as opposed to devices that depend on third-party solutions or software).
- Be mindful of the data being collected by the devices and software you use. This may be time-consuming for a few more years yet, but manually managing device, app and browser regularly will help mitigate some of the risk. Eventually,

AI assistants will be able to manage these settings for you, but we are not quite there yet.

- Protect and audit your home networks regularly: change passwords often.
- Whenever possible, adopt two-factor authentication protocols.

A final observation

The future of human–machine partnerships as they relate to assisting, enhancing and augmenting consumer choices and capabilities is a lot more exciting than worrisome. Despite challenges in areas like data protection and privacy, which could see themselves sorted out by powerful security algorithms, new generations of self-securing chipsets, and AI-powered solutions, almost every aspect of a consumer's life stands to see itself enhanced by smart automation technologies. Shopping will become frictionless and easy whether consumers are in the mood to shop at physical stores and take their time or prefer to have an AI order items for them and have them delivered. Big Butler AIs and digital assistants will easily manage every aspect of consumers' lives that they wish to delegate, from schedules and appointments, and managing bank documents to paying bills, booking vacations and ordering groceries.

If nothing else, consumer-facing human–machine partnerships could easily be almost entirely driven by an overall Big Butler intent. All automation and artificial intelligence solutions designed to serve consumers much in the way that a team of virtual butlers might: organizing their day, running errands, managing routine tasks and chores, managing their schedules, setting appointments, running their household, ordering food, managing package deliveries, recommending entertainment options and being at their users' beck and call. Combined with

Big Mother-inspired solutions that can predict user behaviours, anticipate needs, preselect products based on known preferences, adjust responses and recommendations to match a user's current mood, and even attempt to cheer up users when they are angry, sad or anxious, AIs and smart automation promise to significantly improve and add value to consumers' shopping, travel, lifestyle, leisure, commute and self-improvement experiences. There is a lot to look forward to there.

CHAPTER EIGHT

How technology companies should prepare for the next age of human–machine partnerships

Asking the right questions: do technology companies have a duty to minimize harm in the pursuit of progress?

We now come to a crossroads in our discussion, where practical considerations intersect with philosophical ones. As if the tug-of-war between the boundless opportunities and the innate risks of building a world in which AI and smart automation increasingly take over tasks weren't complicated enough, we now introduce questions of moral responsibility into the equation. This is not an abstraction. It is not a trivial question. As technology companies drive this future by imagining it, designing it, building it, shaping it and profiting from it, they are uniquely responsible for its trajectory and its effects, both wanted and unwanted. And if they are responsible, then it becomes incumbent on them to ensure that the decisions they make take into account the impact they will have on society. Not only the intended good but the unintended harm.

An easy way of not getting lost in an endless philosophical discussion about this is simply to pose the following questions to technology companies: what kind of future are you working to build?

Will it be a future in which individuals are given the tools and agency to make better decisions for themselves and enjoy more freedom to pursue their interests, or a future in which algorithms will be used by insurance providers, educational institutions, banks and enterprises to discriminate against applicants? Will it be a future in which privacy is a right, and consumers are empowered to control what they share and with whom, or a future in which privacy has been replaced by constant surveillance in the name of security and convenience? What kind of future are you trying to build?

Now look at what you are building now, and how you are going about it. Are you really building the future you want to be building? Are you certain that you are on the right track? Are you really addressing risks and unintended side effects with the same passion and diligence as you are addressing the opportunities you see for your inventions? Are you taking your responsibility as seriously as you should?

Technology and responsibility: the duty of not creating monsters

In 2017 and 2018, groups of Amazon and Google employees expressed their concern over their employers possibly allowing governments, law enforcement units and military forces to employ some of their most sophisticated facial recognition and AI-based products. Their worry: that these technologies would be used to cause harm, from giving governments unprecedented surveillance powers to helping them identify, locate and presumably eliminate targets more easily. Not everyone at Google and Amazon was comfortable with the prospect of their company, until then generally concerned with civilian commercial pursuits, becoming a defence contractor and a purveyor of Big Brother surveillance technologies.

This reaction, whether you agree with its sentiment or don't, signals a shift in the role that technology companies will play in the coming decades. As we continue to learn every few weeks, social platforms like Facebook, Twitter and YouTube can be weaponized by hostile actors to spread false information, disseminate propaganda and augment influence operations. Databases can be hacked. Analytics software can be repurposed to create profiles of millions of people, without their knowledge, then target them with customized political messaging, flag them as possible dissidents, or track their online and offline behaviours. As facial recognition technologies improve, smart devices and deep learning tools improve as well and proliferate. One unintended consequence of this proliferation, however, is that technologies that consumers use to stay connected and collaborate with co-workers can be turned against them. Do technology companies have a duty to protect consumers from these potential abuses and threats, or does the responsibility for how their technologies are used fall on users and third parties?

The answer isn't entirely black and white, but it is clear to us that technology companies have a responsibility to ensure that the future they are building doesn't get away from them. Technology companies have a duty to protect their technologies from being misused, or otherwise corrupted, very much in the way that the fictional Dr Victor Frankenstein had a duty not to let his creature run loose and wreak havoc. The villain in Mary Shelley's tale was not, after all, the creature. Had Frankenstein not abdicated his responsibility to keep his creation from causing harm, the story might have turned

Technology companies have a duty to protect their technologies from being misused.

out very differently. There is a parallel to be drawn here that is difficult to ignore.

This is not to say that technology companies should not work with law enforcement and military forces, or that sophisticated new technologies should not be used for crime prevention, public safety and national security purposes. Far from it. Facial recognition technologies can help the appropriate authorities identify and locate missing children and victims of human trafficking. Facial recognition technologies can also help quickly identify a dangerous felon or known terrorist in a crowd before they can cause harm. Deep learning analytical tools can sift through millions of pockets of data and identify patterns, connections, and communications that will thwart a terrorist attack or assassination and can also help bring criminal organizations to justice.

Even less 'sexy' technologies like secure web hosting and IoT security are essential services that civilian companies like Google, Amazon, Microsoft, Qualcomm, Intel and others are uniquely positioned to fulfil. There is a need for technology companies to partner with government agencies to provide an ecosystem of solutions and layers of security that countries now require in the digital age. What we suggest, however, is that technology companies should resist the temptation to think of themselves as merely technology *vendors*, and instead assert themselves as co-equal partners in these relationships. Not by insisting on contractual terms that limit how, where and when government agencies (and third parties) are able to use their products, but by working with legislative and regulatory bodies to proactively develop a framework of company-agnostic rules and laws to prevent abuses and overreach.

Why technology fluency must live at the core of all technology oversight

In Chapter 7, we touched on the need to raise the bar of digital and technological fluency of our leaders and lawmakers. As it is unlikely that the technology literacy problem currently plaguing legislatures and executive branches around the world is likely to solve itself, we call on technology companies to take on the task of advising and educating lawmakers and political leaders. No one else is going to do it, no one else is as uniquely qualified to do it as effectively, and the option to not do it at all, given how important technology already is, is not an option. If technology is going to inform and guide every aspect of our lives, technology companies have a duty to ensure that the individuals entrusted with the drafting of our laws and responsible for representing the interests of the people who elected them are given all of the tools and knowledge they need to effectively perform that most important duty.

In the same vein, to counteract the potential for abuse and undue influence of political leaders that might, as a result of such an advisory scheme, be exerted by certain technology companies, consumer rights and civil rights watchdog organizations should be made co-equal participants in the endeavour, if only to ensure that the interests of consumers and voters always be weighed against the interests of the tech industry.

What we suggest is a process by which technology companies, lawmakers and consumer protection groups come together to debate the pros and cons of each and every technology, and work together to establish both general guidelines and specific laws delineating their proper use. But the absence of this kind of proactive mechanism cannot be allowed to continue. Not if users of technology want to maintain any semblance of control over their own privacy, freedom and agency. And certainly not if technology companies truly care to see the kind of future they originally set out to build come to be.

How to ensure that your Big Butler and/or Big Mother company does not become a Big Brother company

A parallel question to 'what kind of future are you working to build' is 'What kind of company do you want to be in 10 years?

A Big Butler company? A Big Mother company? Or a Big Brother company?' Once again, the question is far from trivial.

Even if every company executive you ask that question to responds with Big Butler and Big Mother, what steps are they taking right now to ensure that they will not accidentally (or negligently) allow themselves to become a Big Brother company? Are they fostering a company culture that is mindful of those three differences? Have they baked an indelible sense of moral duty (such as 'do no harm') into their corporate identity? Are they hiring decision-makers and future leaders accordingly?

If the answer to all of those questions is yes, that's good. If the answer to most or all of those questions is no, then their initial answer was little more than wishful thinking, and no mechanisms are in place to prevent today's Big Butler or Big Mother company from becoming tomorrow's enabler of Big Brother technology abuses. Technology companies *must* start thinking seriously about their duty not to allow the wonderful technologies they build to serve humanity today to become the very instruments of control that will be used to exploit humanity tomorrow. Beyond thinking, they must also act to protect the future they endeavoured to imagine, design and build.

How to apply these philosophical questions to the problem of job loss related to automation

We have spent quite a bit of time throughout this book arguing that human augmentation through AI and smart automation is almost always preferable to human replacement by AI and smart automation. We must acknowledge, however, that not every business owner or decision-maker will have read this book, will agree with its premise, or be able to justify an investment in augmentation when an investment in a replacement solution promises to deliver superior ROI. As discussed in previous chapters, some worker displacement *will* occur. Millions of jobs *will* be lost to automation even if an equal number of new jobs is created because of it, and this must be addressed. Until now, our discussions about job displacement caused by automation have revolved around what *workers* should do to adapt, and what *employers* should do. Let us now discuss the role that *technology companies* might be in a position to play in that equation.

We believe that technology should welcome the opportunity to play a part in helping address the problem of human worker displacement. First, be cautious of the power of popular sayings like 'if you aren't part of the solution, you're part of the problem'. That kind of thinking could easily be weaponized by disenfranchised workers looking for someone to blame for their employment woes and turned against purveyors of smart automation and robotic process automation technologies. Companies that demonstrate that they are part of the solution, not just the problem, will probably reap the benefits of that conveyed sense of good will. But beyond that, at its core, our reasoning is this: every problem is an opportunity to come up with a solution. And every solution has the potential to create benefits for a variety of parties. Why not lay out the problem, and monetize the solution in a way that benefits as many parties as possible?

- For a technology company, those benefits can be translated into business metrics like revenue, profits, positive public sentiment and brand loyalty.
- For local and state governments, these benefits can be technology and educational partnerships aimed at helping displaced human workers acquire new in-demand skills so that unemployment and social safety net expenditures remain manageable.
- For human workers, the benefit is a lifeline to employment through education and reskilling, and for the more enterprising among them, opportunities to leverage new skills to advance their careers rather than merely keep them alive.

- And for companies that have invested in smart automation, the benefit is access to a much richer ecosystem of skilled, specialized and technologically agile workers trained in a variety of tasks ranging from specialized high-volume blue-collar human–machine partnerships to sophisticated new human–AI analytical or decision-making partnerships.

Technology companies are uniquely positioned to drive human worker training, conversion and upskilling for several reasons. The first is that, as developers of new technologies and systems, they enjoy a natural head start against everyone else when it comes to training human workers to use their products. Secondly, pairing human training with technology product sales is a logical shoe-in, as the more workers are fluent in a technology product, the more easily it can scale across an organization.

As a point of note, our research consistently identifies operational agility as one of the most critical traits of high-performing companies in times of digital disruption.[1] The more skilled, trained and ready to hit the ground running a company's operational staff is, the faster it adapts to the introduction of disruptive technologies in their industries. We cannot stress enough just how important this factor is. By being proactive and taking the initiative, technology vendors can, instead of merely providing technology solutions to eager clients and letting them take over from there, also help scale fluency in the use of their products across a market by investing in more upfront user training and certifications.

As a way to combat the socio-economic threat of mass human worker displacement because of smart automation and robotic process automation, governments, industry organizations, NGOs and educational institutions would have every incentive to partner with technology vendors to help fund and facilitate these kinds of worker training mechanisms, *particularly* if those technology vendors developed and lobbied for those programmes themselves. Increased revenues, improved good will, new avenues for market leadership, and more efficiency in human employment: what's not to like?

Important questions to ask

Before going any further, there are some crucial questions that must be answered. Who are we building for? What problems are we trying to solve? What is the most effective way of solving these problems? What is the most elegant way of solving them? How do we minimize harm?

One of the most important questions technology companies can ask themselves is: Who are we building for? The question seems simple on its face, but in a world increasingly driven by technology products, nothing remains simple for very long, and even fundamental questions to which we *thought* we had the answer need to be revisited from time to time.

Example: when a technology company builds a paralegal AI that can sift through legal documents and depositions, looking for keywords and errors 20 times faster than a human law clerk, who is it building that smart automation tool for? Is it building the tool for the law firm's partners? Is it building the tool for individual attorneys? Or is it building the tool for paralegals and law clerks?

In other words, is the company building a product that will automate human work at the firm to eliminate the need for paralegals and law clerks altogether? Or is it building a product that will allow paralegals, law clerks and overwhelmed attorneys at small law firms augment their capabilities with smart automation and robotic process automation tools? The question isn't academic. It's practical. These two products may ultimately have the same capabilities, but depending on who they are meant for, they will be designed and marketed differently. That difference means that it will either drive human augmentation or the replacement of human workers by automation. Who technology products are built for matters.

'Who are we building for?' matters. It matters a lot. A tool must always be designed with its user in mind, no matter what it is. The notion that a technology company builds tools and figures out who its users will be later doesn't track in a world in which every technological tool can have a life or death impact on tens of millions of people. Smart automation is no different, and technology companies have a responsibility to ask themselves who they are building smart automation and robotic process automation tools for, because this informs the purpose of those tools. Are we building tools to help our customers *replace* humans with machines, or are we building tools to help our customers *augment* humans with machines? The question isn't trivial or abstract. Every act of engineering creation is deliberate, and every act of creation comes with its part of responsibility. 'Society' isn't building these tools. 'Demand' is only one factor. Technology solutions designed to replace humans rather than augment them are designed that way on purpose.

A tool must always be designed with its user in mind.

This leads us to another pertinent question that should be asked more diligently: 'What problem are we trying to solve?' As a designer, an engineer, a product manager, this question informs the path that a product concept and its subsequent design will take. When applied to the subject of smart automation and human–machine partnerships, this question tends to become binary by default. Are we looking to replace human workers with a better system (better meaning: faster, more precise, less prone to error, more scalable, tougher, cheaper in the long term, etc), or are we looking to improve the performance of our skilled workforce through technology-based augmentation?

What problem are we *really* trying to solve with this product?

Once that question has been asked and answered, the natural next question is: 'What is the most effective way of solving this problem?' If the problem is that humans don't have the dexterity and endurance to build enough widgets per hour, but machines can, then the answer is simple: replace human workers with machines. If the problem is that humans don't have enough hours in the day to get all of their workloads done, then the answer may be to ask how technology can help handle some of their more tedious and low-value workload. Can a digital assistant be designed to:

- sift through their e-mails and work communications, separate signal from noise, manage automated responses and prioritize and organize communications for them?;
- help them do research and identify key data points and insights while they work on other tasks?;
- automatically generate reports drafted in their voice, complete with data visualizations?;
- help them run virtual models of marketing campaigns, or fleet management expansions, or physical product distribution across a region during high demand periods to identify the best possible plan of action?

Replacing skilled humans with smart automation or robotic process automation only makes sense when it actually makes sense. Replacing skilled humans with smart automation or robotic process automation is a disaster waiting to happen when lazy thinking and craven opportunism aren't checked by sound business acumen. It is important to have an insight into what the ideal solution to a problem is rather than the quickest shortcut through it. The short of it: just because you *can* automate something doesn't mean you *should*. And just because you *think* that a machine can do a human being's work doesn't mean that it actually can.

Another way to look at it: machines aren't designed to do *work* or perform *jobs*. Machines are programmed to perform tasks. Sifting through millions of records, looking for errors isn't a job, it's a task. Scanning a barcode in an airport luggage management system isn't a job, it's a task. Snapping part AB-1876 atop the main nozzle of part ZX-5521 with precisely 0.3 foot-pounds of pressure isn't a job, it's a task. *Tasks* can be automated in the service of jobs. Jobs should not, at least not by default, be entirely automated, unless said jobs were already limited to a handful of easily automated tasks.

All of this to say that a technology company whose product aims to replace millions of doctors and nurses with machines, just because there is money in it, may not be trying to solve a legitimate problem. But even if you are tempted to believe that it does, and that what plagues our healthcare systems today is a gross surplus of useless or otherwise ineffective doctors and nurses, replacing them with machines makes very little sense. Augmenting doctors and nurses with smart automation, robotic process automation, AI and other technologies to improve their effectiveness, however, *does* make sense. This is why technology companies that systematically ask 'who are we building for, what problems are we trying to solve, and what is the most effective way of solving these problems' have the best chance of driving positive change. Among them, those companies that take their process a tiny step further and also ask themselves 'what is the most elegant way of solving these problems' will be far more likely to be the leaders in their respective markets than companies that skip this step altogether.

Designing for the three primary categories of automation solutions: Big Brother, Big Mother and Big Butler

We cannot talk about design intent and the purpose of a technology without circling back to our Big Brother, Big Mother and Big Butler equation. Why? Because if a technology company is purposeful in its product development process, and it knows from the start who the product is designed for, what problems it aims to solve, and how to most effectively solve them, then it stands to reason that the same company can take a step back and ask itself: 'Are we building a product for Big Brother, Big Mother or Big Butler use?'

A technology company that decides to build AI-driven weapons like non-human-directed military drones or offensive algorithmic warfare solutions knows that it is not building Big Butler or Big Mother products. Military contractors are, after all, in a very different kind of business from, say, smart home interface designers, autonomous vehicle experience architects and healthcare VR developers. Some companies will naturally gravitate towards developing offensive uses for new technologies, and there are valid reasons for that, no matter where you may fall on the pacifist-to-warmonger scale, which we don't necessarily need to debate here. Weapons manufacturers don't need to ask themselves if the products they design fall into the category of Big Brother, Big Mother or Big Butler. (We can call their focus *Big Warrior*, to keep things simple.) For everyone else though, the question applies: whether you are an influential technology market leader like Apple, Samsung, Microsoft, Google, Amazon, Intel, Qualcomm, Huawei, any company led by Jeff Bezos or Elon Musk, or a hot new start-up still operating out of a garage, you have a duty to ask yourself if each of your products is designed to be used in a Big Brother, Big Mother or Big Butler capacity.

You have a duty to ask yourself if each of your products is designed to be used in a Big Brother, Big Mother or Big Butler capacity.

Most scalable technologies can be used for all three, but let's not beat around the bush: intent matters. Developing intuitive natural language processing capabilities on the edge to create human-like digital assistants is primarily a Big Butler endeavour. The talking car, the talking home, the talking digital assistant has been a science fiction trope for decades. Can it be corrupted and turned against human users? Certainly. But the key in that possibility is that it involves a corruption of its original intent. Its intent is to serve, to recreate the functionality and experience of a butler, albeit in the digital ether. Facial recognition technologies, however, which allow networked computer systems, camera intelligence and deep learning algorithms to sift through millions of records to be able to simultaneously identify hundreds if not thousands of individuals in crowds, public places or strategic pass-through zones is not intended to duplicate the functionality of a butler. Every purposeful technology, at its inception, is intended to primarily serve in one of three roles (aside from Big Warrior): Big Brother, Big Mother and Big Butler. And because we know this, we can infer that technology companies *choose* to build products specifically for these categories of uses. The decisions to develop them and optimize them for each kind of use is never an accident.

This means that technology companies that develop products for Big Brother uses deliberately choose to do so. Companies that develop products to conduct surveillance on their customers, on their users or on behalf of third parties do not do so accidentally. As this chapter focuses on how technology companies should prepare for the next age of human–machine partnerships, we felt it important to highlight this point. Consumers, taxpayers and citizens will increasingly look to support companies whose innovation is squarely aimed at improving lives and solving critical problems. Companies whose innovation is instead aimed at monetizing the erosion of privacy, enabling the expansion of mass surveillance capabilities, and threatening the future of individual freedoms, run afoul of that preference, and risk being labelled as undesirable. Without naming names, we can all already start drafting short lists of technology companies that are either dangerously close to becoming 'black hat' entities or already squarely deserving of the moniker. Their products are typically characterized by a likelihood of being mentioned in discussions about privacy violations, surveillance, misinformation, propaganda, exploitation and fraud.

Conversely, at the opposite end of the spectrum are 'white hat' technology companies: companies that focus their innovation and product development on improving their users' lives. White hat technology companies can work on a broad range of projects like developing faster smartphones to rebuilding failing coral reefs, from designing companion robots to developing drought-resistant crops, from developing life-like VR experiences for entertainment companies to curing cancer.

Whether white hat technology companies and products are for-profit or not-for-profit is irrelevant. What matters is that these types of technologies, which are intended to solve problems, perform tasks in the service of their users, and improve positive outcomes, are not designed to cause harm, or exploit their users, or profit from deliberate breaches of their users' trust. Even if unintended side effects and secondary impacts are sometimes negative, these technology products are designed to *improve* lives and the world in some way. And looking around the world today, we see no shortage of opportunities to use technology to solve problems, improve lives, do good, and, if you are into that, get rich in the process.

All of this to say that technology companies have a choice as to what sorts of products they design, monetize and scale. And so, every technology company *chooses* to join the ranks of other exploitative and predatory Big Brother companies, or instead to play a part in the shaping of a kinder, brighter, freer world driven by benevolent Big Butler and Big Mother technologies. Given how many legitimate problems need fixing, and how ultimately self-defeating black hat endeavours historically have been from the beginning of time, our advice to the vast majority of technology companies, big and small, is to focus their product design and technology innovation efforts on Big Butler and Big Mother use cases, and to make a conscious, deliberate decision, as innovators, as decision-makers, as executives, as boards of directors and even as investors, to reject any and all calls, internal or external, to engage in the development and pursuit of Big Brother technology products. The long-term damage they always cause to industries, corporate reputations and to users, isn't worth the short-term gains that inspire them in the first place.

For technology companies today, this insight isn't just about reframing the trajectory and intent of their product strategy, or about investing in their long-term survival. It is also intended to help inform how they will build influence, relevance and value from within the broader technology ecosystem for decades to come. Black hat or white hat: that is the dichotomy. As a company, the decisions you make today and tomorrow, and the day after that, will determine whether the next decade or two (or three) will see you branded as a hero or a villain of the technology and business worlds. Why be a villain when you can just as easily be a hero?

Fear and loathing in machine learning: why designing for augmentation rather than automation might make more sense, at least for now

The decision to design technology solutions specifically to augment rather than replace humans is no trivial matter. On some level, it is as much a philosophical choice as it is a practical one. It isn't easy for a CEO or an inventor, or a product manager, to champion human–machine partnerships when market forces lean towards across-the-board automation. If a call centre can be automated, why bother with customer service representative augmentation? If a genetic research lab can be automated, why bother with researcher augmentation? If an entire advertising agency can be automated, why bother with creative augmentation?

It's a serious question, and it becomes all the more serious when automation starts to add a lot of black to a balance sheet that was trending towards a lot more red. And if that isn't serious enough, automation can look mightily attractive when specialized AIs can be just as creative and technically competent as their human counterparts. If software can create ads that are just as creative and effective as humans can, but on a much larger and personalized scale, and software can resolve customer service calls faster and more pleasantly than humans can, and automated genetic research labs can do in one week what a human-staffed lab would have taken six months to achieve, why not just automate everything that can be?

Cost reductions, accelerated timelines, improved outcomes… If that is the result of automation, if that is the most effective way to solve challenges of cost, time and results, why fight it? Why fight for a hybrid human–machine partnership model instead of surrendering to an autonomous machine model?

The answer is simple: because smart automation isn't that good yet, and it won't be any time soon. The gap between how we would like smart automation to work and how it actually works in the real world is still enormous. Even the most sophisticated AIs in the world today have trouble with initiative, creative problem-solving, abstract thinking and bias. They can be programmed and taught to perform certain tasks, and to optimize those tasks, but they can only deviate from their own programming and experience so much.

Cultural subtleties like accents, turns of phrase, tone, cultural references, specific word choices, verbal and non-verbal cues are still far too complex for most machines to detect, let alone properly interpret. While AIs are beginning to learn how to correlate facial expressions and emotions, we are still a long way from machines understanding the meaning of emotion and mood and tone relative to the substance of a conversation. An AI, for instance, cannot effectively 'read the room' during a meeting in which subtle concerns and displeasures and innuendo of a client might be communicated to a project team. Most AIs are still incapable of detecting sarcasm or dry humour with any effective consistency. This makes machines incapable of effectively collaborating with humans on a level sufficiently sophisticated to *replace* a human being on a project team. That is why AIs can be leveraged to *augment* human team members, and subsequently *augment* project teams by taking on specific tasks for their human counterparts, but they cannot *replace* a human being as an equal collaborator. That is why we mostly talk about AIs and bots in terms of assistants and administrators rather than colleagues and collaborators.

We are all aware of instances of AIs beating humans at chess (IBM's Deep Blue),[2] Jeopardy (IBM's Watson),[3] and Uno (Google's AlphaGo),[4] of AIs creating their own recipes (IBM's Watson again)[5] and television commercials,[6] and of AIs outperforming skilled human workers in a variety of professional tasks. And there is a reason for that: technology must be showcased. Investments in research and development have to be justified. The public and investors have to be reminded of the progress that smart and autonomous technologies are making year after year. We have to be wowed. We have to be reminded to dream and believe in the future of technology. That is all fine and good, and we are just as excited about these PR events as anyone, but it is important to bear in mind that while they showcase the emerging capabilities of AIs in specific, controlled, predictable environments, they are not necessarily indicative of these technologies' capability gaps – gaps that matter in the real world of messy, unpredictable chaos, which humans are better equipped to operate in.

In other words, just because an AI can create an award-winning TV ad doesn't mean AIs can replace an entire creative department at an ad agency. Likewise, just because an AI can create recipes doesn't mean it can manage a kitchen, let alone a restaurant. And here, we come to a realization that often escapes businesspeople when they are pitched by technology companies marketing smart or intelligent automation products: reality isn't a best-case scenario. How a product works in an office, in a plant, or out in the field isn't how it works in a showroom or during a staged demo. An intelligent automation product that works the way it is supposed to under predictable conditions is the price of entry. It's the way smart automation fails to adapt to unexpected stressors as easily as humans that will eat into your operational efficiency and ability to automate complex tasks previously handled by humans.

Bias is a perfect example of AIs' inability to compete against human judgement in complex and chaotic environments. Amazon learned this the hard way when it started realizing in 2015 that a machine learning tool it was using to review job applicants' resumés was not rating applicants in an unbiased, 'gender-neutral' way.[7] Part of the problem, Amazon eventually realized, was that many of the keywords that the AI had trained itself to favour when crawling through resumés were predominantly masculine. The tool was eventually side-lined, and much of the story, once the press got hold of it, focused on its obvious bend towards gender bias. In reality, gender bias was only part of the broader AI bias on display in this example. The AI had also reportedly trained itself to attach too much importance to certain resumé keywords, possibly at the expense of identifying more relevant skills and experience. In short, the AI could be gamed by job applicants with the right keywords in their resumé but potentially lacking some of the critical skills, experience and personality traits that Amazon was actually looking for.

Bias is a perfect example of AIs' inability to compete against human judgement.

In the same vein, bias can find its way into any artificial intelligence product, either deliberately or accidentally.[8] A few examples. A business analytics AI developed or otherwise programmed by cost accountants could be plagued by a bias towards favouring cost-cutting measures, at the expense of other strategies for operational improvement, and therefore provide decision-makers with a disproportionate amount of cost-cutting rather than operational improvement advice. Likewise, an AI originally developed to help for-profit companies assess investment risks, subsequently being

applied by governments and NGOs to perform policy risk management analysis might gauge risk in a way that is not appropriately
calibrated for government and NGO use. The problem with bias
in artificial intelligence applications is that it is still exceedingly
difficult to detect, let alone correct, and it is rampant.

Consider the implications of AI bias on hiring decisions, law
enforcement behaviours, healthcare investments, loan application decisions, investment banking strategy, sentencing and
parole recommendations, medical insurance coverage decisions
and educational sponsorship decisions. Consider how bias
against people of colour might accidentally (or deliberately)
make its way into an algorithm, and create injustice, at scale, by
a biased AI model. The same kind of bias zeroing-in on gender,
religion, nationality, weight, height, age, annual income, place of
birth, net worth, highest educational level reached, medical
history, musical tastes, political views, and a slew of other factors
could corrupt an AI and create enormous disruptions and injus-
tices in critical systems we all rely on to be impartial, or at the
very least *just*. AI biases could increase rather than decrease
discrimination, put vulnerable populations at greater risk, limit
access to indispensable resources, restrict opportunities and rob
companies, municipalities and entire economies of billions of
dollars of untapped potential.

Looking beyond the broader societal implications of the AI bias
problem, let us now apply the same problem to common business
functions and task-specific applications. An AI programmed to
favour some outcomes over others, based on a programmer's or
user's own sets of biases, could misinterpret data, misjudge the
value of some sets of outcomes over others, and ultimately make
poor decisions. An AI trained to value cost reductions instead of
growth, for example, could steer a company towards reductive
business decisions rather than expansive ones. Likewise, an AI
trained to be risk-averse might steer a company towards safe
choices rather than towards riskier but potentially more profitable
choices. In both of these instances, an AI might rob a company of

its potential for growth, discourage it from pursuing breakthrough products, steer it away from visionary strategies, and even dissuade it from bold mergers and acquisitions – the precise opposite advice that it might presently need.

Similar problems appear when we attempt to apply decision-making to autonomous vehicles and combat drones. In the event of an accident or a missile strike, how does a machine decide who to kill and who to spare? How does a machine decide which innocent bystanders should live and which innocent bystanders should die? How does the machine choose? How does the calculus work? The simple answer is this: the decision should not be the machine's to make. The machine's job is to analyse and advise but not to make the decision. And if the machine is tasked with taking action autonomously, the parameters under which it does so should be pre-programmed by a human user.

Why does this matter, and how is this applicable to business uses of AI? Consider the question of an autonomous vehicle having to decide who to protect in the event of an unavoidable accident. Say that it gets cut off by another vehicle and cannot come to a stop in time to avoid causing humans serious injury. Its two choices are: a) veer left and smash into a wall, possibly killing its occupants; or b) veer right and smash into a crowd of pedestrians, saving its occupants but possibly killing the pedestrians. How does the vehicle decide? How does it weigh the pros and cons of each decision? How does it assign value to one life over another? How does it overcome bias?

AIs are not meant to make decisions for humans.

The simple answer is: it doesn't. It shouldn't. The choice should be pre-made for it, either by the car manufacturer, the user or appropriate legislation. What is important is that technology companies, when creating AI and smart automation products, should remember that AIs are not meant to make decisions for humans. They are meant to *assist* humans in making better decisions, and *augment* their ability to do so.

Technology companies should therefore build AI and smart automation solutions with a focus on assisting and augmenting human decision-making users first, prompting humans to fill as many of the decision-making gaps as possible, and on mimicking human decision-making only as a backup capability. This means that AI and smart automation products geared towards helping humans make better decisions should be designed with human–machine interactions and partnerships as the default, rather than decision-making autonomy as the default.

One final observation. Regardless of what tools they build, and to what purpose, technology companies need to pay particular attention to the value of trust. When it comes to technology investments, users – whether they are consumers, corporate clients, government agencies or academic institutions – value trust above all else. As user interfaces and user experience design become commoditized, and all technology solutions built around AI interfaces become intuitive and natural to interact with, the key differentiator for technology companies will not be performance or speed or slick design, but trust. *Trust* that their data will be kept safe. *Trust* that their privacy will be secure. *Trust* that their information will not be sold to third parties. *Trust* that they are the customers and not the product.

One of the ways to earn that trust will be to build products intended for Big Mother and Big Butler uses – products entirely in the service of their users, with no ulterior motives, full transparency and fully customizable opt-in and opt-out permissions.

Beyond trust, building products and solutions that *empower* as many users as possible rather than *disenfranchise* them, seems like the ultimate strategy for technology companies looking to establish dominance in this space over the course of the next two decades.

CHAPTER NINE

The future of human–machine partnerships

Putting it all together

Reframing the discussion: automation is not the enemy... as long as we don't make it our enemy

We began this book with a simple question: 'Will a machine take away my job?' The answer, as we have discovered, is not that simple. Whether or not your job is taken over by a machine depends on a number of factors, among them your occupation, physical location, employment arrangement, level of education, access to training, and the speed with which smart automation that can realistically do your job can be deployed and utilized cost-effectively enough.

For employers, while the prospect of automating as many tasks as possible may initially look promising – at least on paper – the reality of injecting automation into business operations is anything but simple. Technology is expensive. Technology is imperfect. Change is messy. The difficulty to change and keep pace with disruption, to adapt to innovation that occurs at breakneck speed, is one of the business world's most frustrating challenges. If change is hard, adaptation is harder. And even when organizations manage to crack the code of operational agility, and learn to confidently navigate the treacherous waters of digital transformation, technology, more often than not, falls short of expectations.

Will a machine take away your job? Maybe. But that is the wrong question. Globalization might take away your job. An employer relocating to another part of the country might take away your job. Your employer being acquired by a rival company might take away your job. A million things can take away your job. Worrying about a robot or a machine taking your job is a bit like being lost at sea, and worrying about being eaten by a 30-foot shark: dozens of things are likely to kill you before a giant shark decides to hop out of the water to swallow you whole. The business world is no different.

Having said that, it would be naïve to pretend that AI, RPA (robotic process automation), the IoT and smart automation will not displace millions of human workers, as it already has in previous decades. Some jobs, particularly those limited to a handful of automatable tasks, will likely be taken over by machines over time. Those jobs, whether they consist of traditionally blue-collar, repetitive, manual, routine tasks or white-collar computational routine tasks are statistically most at risk.[1] This is true.

Furthermore, improvements in robotics, machine vision and motion planning have ushered in a new era in warehouse and manufacturing plant automation. This promises to give companies the ability to build and operate fully-automated facilities in which shelves stock themselves, and robots are capable of moving inventory from truck to shelf and from shelf to conveyer belt, to say nothing of their ability to unpack, sort, assemble, pack, stock and ship – all with little to no human intervention. Fully-automated facilities like these will be especially useful in heavily industrialized areas, distribution centres, e-commerce warehouses, and pretty much anywhere that items are stocked, picked, packed and shipped.

Whether as many as half of all machine operators and assembly jobs in the US could be at risk by the mid-2030s is a credible prediction or not is irrelevant.[2] It doesn't even matter if reality ultimately leans more towards 10 per cent or 80 per cent. We all need to start thinking about how to *adapt* to whatever changes the next era of automation brings to our society and economy, what kinds of opportunities and risks we are likely to *face* as a result, and use those insights to help *shape* the kind of future we will all, one way or another, collectively share.

A vision of the future of automation that we can all benefit from

Instead of obsessing about all of the pain and friction that automation may unleash over the course of the next few decades, it might be helpful to instead spend a few moments discussing what an ideal future augmented by smart automation might actually look like. This is not meant to be an exercise in futurism, optimism or fantasist projection. The point of this exercise is perhaps to gain a better understanding of where we may want to steer automation in order to maximize its benefits and minimize its downsides.

Our objective is not to paint a rosy picture of the future, but rather to reframe the goals, outcomes and direction that we may wish to keep in mind when making decisions about when, where and how to invest in automation. You don't build a house without a blueprint or a plan, after all. It may not be a bad idea also to have a blueprint and a plan in mind with regard to the role that automation will play in our everyday lives. And yet, there is currently no plan, no roadmap, no real discussion on a national or global level, no legislative action being drafted. Perhaps a little clarity of vision today might help us avoid major problems down the road.

Let us start at the beginning. The purpose of smart automation, like every tool ever invented, is not merely to improve efficiency and cut costs, but to *enhance* and *augment* human capabilities. In every era of human progress marked by a transition to automation, automation's aim was ultimately to make it possible for workers who had until then been doing unnecessarily difficult, dangerous and unrewarding work, to move into occupations that would improve their quality of life and their income potential.

Automation liberates headcount potential. Workers who used to punch holes by hand transition to operating a hole-punching machine. Hole-punching machine operators then

Automation liberates headcount potential.

transition to supervising automated hole-punching machines. Automated hole-punching machine supervisors then transition into systems management or automated operations management. Thus, every successive wave of automation is intended to move human workers away from low-value roles and into incrementally higher-value roles. The same human worker, by virtue of augmentation through automation, becomes more valuable over time because the tasks he is now free to perform are more valuable.

The same is true of business managers. One of the most precious resources of any manager or decision-maker is time. At the start of any workday, a manager probably has a plan of action, a schedule that includes meetings, conference calls, deliverables, visits to this and that part of the operation, research, analysis, reporting work and so on. By mid-morning, that schedule has probably already fallen apart because of an unexpected crisis (or several) and now our manager's day will be spent putting out fires and handling unexpected crises.

Here, we are confronted with two versions of how a manager's time is spent on any given day. The official 'on paper' schedule, which only works consistently well in theory, and the real-world schedule, in which there isn't enough time to complete every planned and unplanned task. Fact: the day-to-day operations of any business will, more often than not, rob managers of the most precious resource they have – time. Injecting automation in the right places and in the right manner helps address this problem. And when automation is successfully applied to this particular challenge, what happens? That manager once again is given the time to handle tasks that matter most. That increases the value of that manager to an organization.

What this tells us is that automation is at its most valuable when it enhances and augments human potential. Displacement is merely another word for adaptation. Displacement should never mean *replacement*. To replace a human worker with a machine without giving them the opportunity to take on a new, automation-adjusted role that will complement the machine's task, is short-sighted and ultimately self-defeating. Replacing a human workforce with machines instead of using machines to enhance a human workforce reflects a fundamental misunderstanding of the true potential of automation. Cost-cutting alone doesn't build companies. Sooner or later, you run out of fat to trim. Then what? Companies that seek the right balance of efficiency, innovation, risk-taking, execution and outward-facing focus, however, tend to adapt and grow with more consistency than those that focus exclusively on cost-cutting and other reductive inward-facing strategies.

> *Displacement should never mean replacement.*

CASE STUDY Examples of transition to mass automation

From top to bottom, a transition to mass automation might look like as follows. The reader should jump ahead to the example that speaks to his or her own personal circumstance best.

Decision-makers

Can leverage AIs, intuitive analytics, cognitive computing, predictive algorithms and recommendation engines to:

- identify threats and opportunities;
- quantify them;
- model hypothetical scenarios;
- mitigate risks;
- ultimately improve and facilitate decision-making.

Senior managers

Can leverage AIs, big data analytics, robotic process automation, and digital assistants to:

- help them better manage their time;
- organize, analyse and contextualize data;
- monitor business unit performance in real time;
- virtually model future business performance;
- generate reports;
- craft presentations;
- help them prepare for meetings;
- manage budgets and financial activities;
- facilitate collaboration and coordination with peers;
- help hit targets, meet goals and deliver desired outcomes.

Middle managers and team leads

Can leverage AIs, digital assistants, bots, data analytics, smart automation and intuitive collaborative tools to:

- streamline collaboration;
- automate project management scheduling and tasks;
- identify qualified resources within the organization;
- adjust project timelines;
- assign additional resources to projects as needed;
- manage budgets;
- automate data analysis and reporting;
- monitor performance;
- handle quality control tasks;
- identify areas of possible improvement and risk;
- recommend ideal courses of action;
- trigger alerts to bring attention to a potential problem;
- gamify team performance.

Specialized employees

Can leverage AIs, digital assistants, bots, task management tools and intuitive collaborative tools to:

- design–build automated workflows;
- streamline collaboration with co-workers;
- synchronize schedules and the status of deliverables around the clock;
- identify potential bottlenecks and problem areas before they happen;
- automate quality control tasks;
- create custom reports and dashboards;
- automate upskilling and training scheduling;
- automate document and deliverable production;
- virtually model and test prototypes and ideas.

Engineers

Can leverage AIs, digital assistants, bots, virtualization tools, robotic process automation, 3D scanning tools, and machine learning algorithms to:

- design, prototype, test and order parts, materials and finished products faster and at a much lower cost than ever before.

Architects and civil engineers

Can leverage virtualization tools, IoT technologies, big data, cloud and edge computing, machine learning, cognitive computing and AIs to:

- plan, design, build, maintain, and upgrade buildings, infrastructure, utilities and their grids, and smart cities.

Plant managers

Can leverage IoT, technologies, cloud and edge computing, robotic process automation, machine learning, virtualization tools and AI to:

- plan, design, build, manage, optimize and upgrade warehousing, manufacturing, assembly and distribution operations.

Plant and maintenance technicians

Can leverage IoT technologies, cloud and edge computing, robotic process automation, machine learning, virtualization tools, AR and AI to:

- work symbiotically alongside automated systems;
- keep them operating at maximum efficiency;
- troubleshoot and repair systems currently failing or about to fail;
- supervise and monitor system performance;
- minimize downtime and improve output.

Educators

Can leverage, VR, AR, virtualization tools, IoT technologies, smart automation, machine learning, and AI to:

- automate and customize lesson plans;
- create interactive content;
- create and administer tests and quizzes;
- analyse the weaknesses and strengths of each student;
- identify areas of potential improvement for each student;
- generate homework assignments customized to the needs of each student;

THE FUTURE OF HUMAN−MACHINE PARTNERSHIPS

- provide students with AI-based tutoring and additional learning assistance;
- manage individual student's learning challenges;
- provide each and every student with all of the attention and support that one teacher alone cannot provide.

Law enforcement agencies

Can leverage the IoT, big data, cloud and edge computing, deep learning, cognitive computing, machine learning, robotic process automation, AI and drones to:

- flag clusters of online and offline behaviours that suggest an imminent mass shooting, major crime or terrorist attack;
- flag suspicious transactions and money transfers;
- identify wanted criminals and suspects in crowds;
- track wanted criminals and suspects' movements and activities online and offline;
- identify and locate missing and exploited children;
- assign additional resources to high-crime areas as needed;
- function as an always-on automated entry network of fixed and mobile technologies;
- notify nearby responders that a yet-unreported crime may be in progress;
- augment the real-time capabilities of officers on the ground.

Specialized white-collar occupations (eg lawyers and accountants)

Can leverage AI, machine learning, robotic process automation and digital assistants to:

- automate workflows, billing, appointment scheduling, quality control, document analysis, complex search queries, depositions and fact-finding tasks;
- manage filings and filing schedules;
- monitor the process of cases.

Physicians

Can leverage AI, machine learning, the IoT, VR, AR, digital assistants, cloud and edge computing, big data, DNA analysis and robotic process automation to:

- assist them in delivering accurate diagnoses, recommending treatment options, identifying lowest-risk and highest-risk drug treatments, facilitating remote care;
- facilitate the day-to-day management of outpatient treatment;
- monitor outpatient health and recovery progress;
- make remote adjustments to prosthetics and other medical devices;
- identify genetic and lifestyle predispositions to potential health risks;
- detect and identify health problems much sooner than they used to in the past.

Surgeons

Can leverage AI, machine learning, AR, VR, virtualization and robotics to:

- improve the survivability of surgeries;
- minimize trauma and scarring from surgeries;
- shorten patient recovery time;
- improve outcomes;
- augment the capabilities of emergency field hospitals.

Nurses, homecare and hospice care technicians

Can leverage robotics, AI, IoT technologies, machine learning, and smart automation to:

- manage more patients;
- increase their monitoring footprint and presence;
- improve quality of care;
- monitor sudden and steady changes in patient health;
- easily communicate with patients remotely;
- ensure that the right prescription medication is taken at the right time and in the right dosage;

- track and monitor patient vitals;
- monitor changes in patients' mood and behaviour;
- respond more quickly to health emergencies;
- help patients live with more autonomy and dignity.

Administrators of all stripes

Can leverage AI, machine learning, cognitive computing, digital assistants and bots to:

- automate billing, shipping, scheduling, restocking, database queries, patient records management, client and customer records management, logistics, cargo manifests, recordkeeping, etc.

Farmers

Can leverage IoT technologies, robotic process automation, drones, machine learning, cloud and edge computing, and AR to:

- better understand and predict weather patterns;
- monitor the nutrient and moisture content of their soil;
- optimize crop planning, field orientation, scheduling and resource management;
- automate payments, financial transactions and the management of all IP licensing;
- monitor and track the location and health of cattle;
- plan and manage pesticide and herbicide use;
- automate farm machinery;
- find, vet and hire seasonal workers;
- monitor market fluctuations;
- provide financial planning advice.

IT professionals

Can leverage machine learning, cloud and edge compute, cognitive computing, big data, robotic process automation and AI to:

- automate workflows;
- manage license portfolios;

- initiate patches and upgrades;
- recommend new tools and solutions;
- identify problem areas and security vulnerabilities;
- optimize performance;
- create intuitive dashboards and reports;
- flag suspicious activity;
- shut down hackers and intruders;
- assist users with training and best-practice insights;
- quickly build new tools and capabilities for a broad range of human users.

Retailers

Can leverage IoT technologies, big data, machine learning, AI, AR, 3D printing and RPA to:

- deliver seamless omnichannel experiences for their customers;
- accelerate ordering and transactions for customers who prefer to buy items than to shop for them;
- be able to quickly identify and greet individual customers by name during their visits;
- bake individual user preferences into each customized customer interaction;
- better understand customer behaviours and tastes;
- deliver remarkable experiences;
- optimize inventory planning and control;
- increase a location's product customization capabilities;
- replace marketing noise and ill-timed offers with well-timed offers with the highest probability of conversion;
- eliminate all transactional and payment friction;
- secure all customer data and transactions;
- move human employees into relationship-building and positive customer interaction roles.

Customer service professionals

Can leverage AI, machine learning, big data and robotic process automation to:

- shorten the amount of time it takes to understand, address and resolve customer complaints, questions, and requests for assistance;
- assist a customer service team by automating customer triage automation and FAQ response testing, managing search queries, prompting tech support as needed, and recommending possible answers to the problem or question.

Human resources managers

Can leverage machine learning, robotic process automation, AI, digital assistants, bots, big data and cognitive computing to:

- identify, vet, and evaluate potential hires;
- predict whether or not job applicants will be a good fit for a particular position or team environment;
- identify areas of strength and weakness in employees' professional and professional-adjacent skillsets;
- recommend additional training and mentoring to address areas of potential improvement;
- deliver that training and incentivize participation through gamification and other incentives;
- help guide, shape and manage every employee's development journey;
- monitor the performance and progress of all employees;
- identify at-risk employees and employees possibly considering an exit;
- identify high-value and low-value employees to determine which warrant an investment in corrective action and which do not, etc.

Commercial drivers

Can leverage autonomous vehicle technology, IoT technologies, AI, big data, cloud and edge computing, robotic process automation, AR and even drones to:

- optimize route-planning;
- minimize the risk of traffic accidents and collisions;
- speed up 'last-metre' or 'last-yard' kerbside deliveries;
- facilitate in-route resupply and restocking by drone or autonomous vehicle;
- allow workers to take breaks and rest while their vehicle is in transit.

That is as wide a net as we have the room to cast in this chapter. We could go on, but one of the objectives of that exercise was to highlight the fact that the more you look at different use cases in which these technologies augment, enhance and assist human workers, the more you begin to notice how similar they all seem. White-collar workers, blue-collar workers, high-pay, low-pay, technical occupations, non-technical occupations, all of the human–machine partnerships we just went through are cut from the same cloth: automation used correctly assists, enhances and augments human workers and enables them to be more productive, more efficient, and to deliver more value to their organization and to the economy as a whole.

Compare the above model of human–machine partnerships through automation with a model in which humans would be hypothetically replaced by AIs and robots. What would that look like? CEOs and decision-makers being replaced by decision-making AIs? Where would be the value in that? The same tools that we foresee *assisting* decision-makers in making the right judgement calls, taking the right risks, and making the right bets would not perform better or as well on their own than they would if partnered with a capable, competent human being. Why? Because while machines are outstanding when it comes to computational work, humans easily outclass them when it comes to judgement, context, creativity, abstract thinking, nuance, emotional intelligence, courage, ambition and capacity for vision – all of which are essential components of effective decision-making, leadership and progress.

The same can be said for management roles. Can machines effectively organize project schedules, curate budgets and manage teams? On paper, yes. In reality, even the most sophisticated AI lacks the judgement, emotional intelligence, creativity, social grace and cultural sophistication to motivate employees and make them feel valued, for instance, or to navigate the minefield of interpersonal relationships that injects itself into every human interaction. Machines also still are not able to improvise solutions to every crisis that is the bane of every management role. This critical hurdle is one that AIs will have to overcome if they are to ever replace human managers.

We can go on and on about this, and our conclusion is always the same: an AI can assist and augment but not truly and effectively *replace*, nor should it. An AI can be a terrific specialized assistant that can perform repetitive, routine tasks – even very complex ones – but it is unlikely that AI and smart automation will be able to make up for their inability to mimic the types of human traits and behaviours that allow us to problem-solve in real time and correctly assign context, meaning and value to our decisions and choices in the next decade or two (or three, for that matter). And until such a time as machines can mimic or even surpass human capacity for judgement, creativity, abstract thinking, cultural awareness, empathy, courage, affection, love and even passion, replacing humans with machines seems not only ill-advised but terribly short-sighted. Until then, organizations and individuals should prioritize as much of their automation investments as makes sense on human augmentation rather than human replacement.

What it may take to make automation work at scale for society

Perhaps what we need in order to steer automation towards human–machine partnerships rather than reductive automation, at least at scale, is a set of guidelines or guiding principles. Some sort of legal, institutional, societal framework.

As business and technology analysts, we regularly engage in debates about the role that government regulation and legislation should or should not play in the business world, particularly in areas where disruptive technologies open up vulnerabilities that existing laws – and especially those drafted in pre-industrialized and pre-digital eras – are ill-equipped to address. It is a fact that no one could have seen the industrial revolution coming in the late 1700s. It is also a fact that no lawmaker, prime minister or president in office even 50 years ago could have predicted smartphones, augmented reality, the Internet of Things, social platforms, digital privacy, mobile payments, digital currencies, smart grids, cyberattacks, telemedicine, surgical robots, computer vision, intelligent cameras, autonomous drones, and scores of other technologies that not only help shape the world in which we live today but drive the direction of the world we may live in tomorrow.

Lawmakers (and to a lesser extent government regulators) are woefully unprepared for the technological growing pains that already test the limits of our laws, privacy protections, civil rights, personal safety and economic security. And as bad as those growing pains might seem now, they are likely to grow exponentially more problematic and pressing in the coming years, particularly if automation, instead of being leveraged to mostly augment human workers, is used instead to replace large swathes of them.

The types of guardrails we might consider establishing will depend on the sorts of problems we hope to avoid, and the sorts of outcomes we want to deliver. And in turn, the types of guardrails we may deem appropriate – or at least worthy of consideration – will inform which institutions and remedies we will want to recruit into the effort.

For instance, if we collectively come to the conclusion that automation may initially cause more job displacement – or outright unemployment – than our national and global economic ecosystems can handle, we may want to turn to our regulatory and legislative bodies for redress. Perhaps laws, even temporary ones, to establish specific human-to-machine ratios at companies may become necessary. Perhaps tax incentives may be required to help motivate companies to maintain a certain ratio of humans to machines in the midst of mass automation.

Laws to establish specific human-to-machine ratios may become necessary.

The reason for this is simple: should automation initially lean too hard towards human replacement rather than human augmentation, unemployment may reach critical levels, and a significant percentage of households may find themselves without a pay cheque. According to a 2018 paper by MIT's Daron Acemonglu and Boston University's Pascual Restrepo, every robot added to a zone of economic activity could cost as many as six human jobs.[3] Enter economic slowdown, civil unrest and political instability. It will be up to governments, not private and public businesses, to address this issue.

One solution, floated by a number of political pundits, economists and futurists, is to establish some kind of universal basic income scheme, in which every citizen receives a government cheque to cover basic necessities like rent and food. In some small countries, this may be possible. In a country as populous and spread out as the United States, however, this solution seems improbable. Adding to the challenge of finding the funding for such a scheme is the fact that high unemployment will also rob federal, state and municipal governments of precious tax revenue. (If fewer taxpayers generate an income, income tax revenues suffer and taxpayer-funded programmes shrink.) We find it unlikely that depressed tax revenues can somehow metamorphosize into higher expenditures to help support unemployed citizens. The maths don't really work out.

This particular problem clues us in to a possible solution: taxation. We expect that, should federal, state and municipal tax collectors realize that automation is depriving their treasuries of precious tax revenues, the remedy will naturally be to devise new tax schemes to make up for the shortfall. Naturally, that new taxation model would look to automation – the cause of the problem – as an obvious solution. Tax authorities might then decide it appropriate to tax the use of robots and automation, much in the same way that they traditionally taxed humans. It is not difficult to imagine that a tax authority would be capable of devising a tax structure based on what a robot or machine would have been paid per hour were a human being still in that role.

The resulting solution could therefore be one in which a tax on automation would, on the one hand, make up for shortfalls in tax revenues, and on the other, perhaps balance out the human vs machine cost accounting equation in such a way that replacing a human worker with a machine will make less financial sense than augmenting a human worker with a machine. This is one mechanism that governments and the business community can play with to achieve some kind of balance that benefits everyone, and one that does not impose draconian bans or quotas on businesses and their investors.

We may also see governments offer incentives to companies in order to encourage human–machine partnerships and investments in human worker augmentation and to disincentivize human replacement by machines.

Employers also have a crucial role to play here, either voluntarily of otherwise. As human workers are displaced by automation, employers are the first line of defence against subsequent unemployment or the loss of economic potential of every displaced worker – whichever way you look at it. Does it really make financial or strategic sense to lay off a worker being replaced by a machine, or can the argument be made that retaining the worker and reassigning him makes more financial sense? (Yes, sophisticated analytics tools can help shed some light on the calculus at play. Executives don't have to figure this out on their own.) Could retraining that worker be worth his employer's time? Could even that process be automated. The answer to both of these questions could very well be *yes*.

This reskilling and retasking scheme does not have to be entirely the burden of employers, however. Governments also have a stake in efforts to minimize the negative impact of automation, particularly when it affects employment. This can be particularly true in vulnerable areas where automation leading to high rates of unemployment could depress the local economy. Governments could therefore take on some of the financial burden of reskilling and retasking programmes, and partner with local businesses and regional industries to mitigate the risk of job displacement. They could co-create and co-sponsor educational opportunities, training programmes, job placement services, and even provide relocation assistance and incentives for displaced workers and workers at risk of being displaced. One of the most important aspects of programmes of this sort is that they should be forward-looking and proactive. Another is that they should be managed locally rather than on a national or federal level.

Reasoning: we already know which types of occupations are most at risk of being displaced by automation. Why wait until workers have been displaced to start retraining, upskilling and trying to retask them? Why wait until they have fewer options and less time to adapt to change? Companies and governments should take the initiative and look to address this challenge now, while workers have more options and more flexibility to prepare for change. The cost of preparing workers for displacement when they are gainfully employed is logically less than the cost of retraining them *and* helping them pay their bills at the same time.

Part of the problem, at least historically, with employee retraining programmes is that they were ill-devised and poorly managed. For instance, according to the United States Department of Labor's Bureau of Labor Statistics, at the height of the wave of automation that swept through the US in the mid-1990s, the average worker working for a company of more than 50 employees was shown to have received less than 10.7 hours of training per six-month period.[4]

Per the survey:[5]

- 'During the 6-month reference period, smaller establishments (50–99 employees) provided less formal training to their employees on average (6 hours per employee) than establishments with 100–499 employees (12.1 hours per employee) or with 500 or more employees (12.0 hours per employee).'
- 'Employees in smaller establishments also participated in the fewest formal training activities.'
- 'The industries that provided the most hours of formal training were transportation, communications and public utilities; finance, insurance, and real estate; and mining (18, 17 and 14 hours per employee, respectively).'
- 'Establishments in retail trade and construction provided the fewest hours of formal training per employee (4 and 5 hours, respectively).'
- 'More hours of computer training (2.1 hours per employee) were provided than any other type of formal job-skills training. Professional/technical training and production/ construction-related training were the next most frequent types of formal training, with about 1 hour of training per employee for each type.'

It should be noted that this data was collected while the JTPA (the Job Training Partnership Act of 1982) was still in effect. This programme, which was specifically aimed at helping retrain labour to offset displacement and unemployment caused by automation, spent roughly $3 billion dollars annually between 1984 and 1998.[6] We can clearly see from these numbers how woefully inadequate this programme was at providing workers with an adequate amount of training and reskilling.

We can derive several lessons from the failures of this and other programmes like it. The first is that no training programme, regardless of scope, spend and best intentions, is a magic pill. Training programmes can only achieve so much, and if the retraining, reskilling and subsequent relocation assistance that make them up do not serve the needs of emerging industries, they will fail to deliver the desired outcome, at least at scale. The second lesson is that federal and national programmes, for a variety of reasons, can sometimes look great on paper but fail to deliver results on the ground. Thirdly, while federal and national funding should certainly be used to help industries, states and municipalities deliver jobs training programmes, how that money is applied to the problem may be best left to local committees made up of workers, employers and educators than to policymakers. But perhaps most importantly, what we notice about the failure of programmes like the JTPA is the fact that they did not leverage automation nearly as much as they should.

In defence of the JTPA, training automation was not as sophisticated in the 1980s and '90s as it is today. More recent incarnations of that programme, from the Workforce Innovation and Opportunity Act to the Better Education and Skills Training for America's Workforce Act, however, don't appear to recommend or emphasize training automation nearly as much as they perhaps should, if at all. Given the potential for automation and AI-assisted job training opportunities in the pursuit of helping human workers prepare for career displacement resulting from automation (irony again), we feel that the solution to the problem may be found in the problem itself. If automation is to displace a certain percentage of workers in the next two decades, automation can also be the solution to their retraining and retasking transition.

Perhaps one of the ways that national and state legislatures could help offset the cost of these programmes, as well as hold employers accountable for any automation investment decisions that may ultimately result in higher rates of unemployment, is to require that every employer above a certain size contribute a fixed annual sum to partially fund retraining for all employees, and commit to the funding and delivery of a minimum number of training hours required to properly retrain a displaced worker. Whether that training ultimately takes place before or after the displacement, or some mix of both, is irrelevant to the commitment itself.

Lastly, labour unions may yet play a part in this adjustment period, particularly in countries where they exert significant influence over legislatures and regulatory institutions.

These solutions do not address other threats to employment like globalization, but they help us start the discussion and identify areas that may warrant exploration. Whatever the remedy, or mix of remedies, we need to have a serious policy and regulatory discussion about automation and the risks that its misuse (or rather *injudicious* use) over the next two to three decades may pose to our economies' health, to our societies' stability and the pursuit of progress. If we do not steer automation towards the kinds of outcomes we wish to enjoy, there is no telling where we may accidentally end up. Ironically, the kind of analysis, predictive modelling, and AI-powered recommendation capabilities that we have spent most of this book discussing are precisely the types of human augmentation technologies that could help us plan for the years ahead. Again, the potential for a human–machine partnership to help humanity solve a serious problem works its way into our discussion. We don't have to guess at this sort of thing any more. We have tools available to us that can help us avoid problems before they get out of hand.

Big Brother, Big Mother, and Big Butler: why designing the future matters, and why we cannot afford to leave intent to chance

Understanding that every technology can either be weaponized into a Big Brother use case or applied to benevolent purposes through Big Mother and Big Butler use cases is a good start.

By being able to separate benevolent from predatory uses of technology, we can begin to divide technology use cases between wanted and unwanted technology uses. This allows us to make decisions about how technology should, and shouldn't, be used. These decisions can inform our posture, as citizen and policy-makers, as to what technology uses should be legal and which ones should not be legal, and which technology uses should be allowed to proliferate freely vs which technology uses should be carefully supervised and restricted.

As informed consumers, decision-makers and policy influencers we may want to consider applying deliberate and constant pressure on technology companies, technology implementers, regulators, legislators and government agencies to ban – or at least severely restrict – Big Brother uses of technology. These uses include intrusive surveillance tools, privacy-intrusion tools, and pretty much any nefarious or otherwise predatory use of technology.

This isn't an abstraction. There is nothing trivial about it. The proliferation of Big Brother uses of technology is already a growing problem, and will continue to be a problem if we do not collectively address it.

Reality check: human–machine partnerships can be corrupted and used to cause harm. We already know that human hackers can use computers and algorithms to perpetrate attacks against critical infrastructure targets and individuals. We also know that private security and data analysis firms can leverage digital technologies to surveil, harass, threaten and coerce targets. Even government agencies can, if they choose to, abuse digital technologies like facial recognition algorithms, location services, and even smart speakers and smart devices to spy on civilians and violate their privacy. These uses of technology and others like them need to be addressed, more clearly understood and proactively regulated.

The proliferation of Big Brother uses of technology is already a growing problem.

On the one hand, the objective of this exercise is *not* to keep facial recognition and other snooping technologies out of the hands of government agencies, but rather to limit and regulate their use in faithful accordance to the spirit of civil rights and privacy laws that preceded the invention of these technologies. Still today, the courts are not entirely clear on warrant and probable cause requirements guiding the use of many electronic surveillance technologies. Elaborate CCTV networks equipped with facial recognition software and connected to a vast database of searchable photographs can just as easily be used by a benevolent state to automate the process of looking for missing persons as they can be used by a repressive state to automate the tracking, monitoring and surveillance of tens of thousands of suspected dissidents. The difference between these two use cases isn't the technology itself but the laws that guide the technology's use. We must therefore turn to our legislatures and the courts to help protect us from Big Brother uses of powerful new technologies including smart automation. This is not something that we can passively hope will happen. This must be tackled with more urgency and consistency than it has been until now.

In a similar vein, it may not be a bad idea to ask that surveillance technologies marketed to consumers under the guise of Big Mother and Big Butler product features be more closely regulated.

For instance, if a human user opts into allowing their digital assistant to listen to their conversations and phone calls; track their movements, habits, and purchases; and analyse the data it collects on them, with the explicit purpose of better understanding and anticipating their needs (a mix of Big Mother and Big Butler intent), the technology company behind this tool should perhaps not be allowed to collect that data and have access to it for any purpose not explicitly opted into by that user. That data should not be accessible by human beings working for that company or any third party working with that company. That data should not be allowed to be resold or shared without the user's consent. Any unsolicited use of any part of that data or information by the company or a third party should be communicated in real time to the user. Additionally, any possible breach or unauthorized access of the user's data should also result in immediate notification of the user.

This should apply to companies like Google, Facebook and Amazon, which are all increasingly embedded in the digital and omnichannel experiences of hundreds of millions (if not billions) of users. The same privacy protections discussed here should also apply to any other technology company whose products are marketed as Big Mother and Big Butler tools. Whether you are Google or Microsoft, Amazon or Apple, Facebook or Uber, Samsung or General Electric, Toyota or Bose, products meant to be applied exclusively to Big Mother and Big Butler use cases should not be allowed to collect user data and invade user privacy without their users' explicit consent. If market forces alone are not enough to keep technology companies and their implementers from opaquely applying Big Mother and Big Butler products to Big Brother uses, courts and legislators will have to step in.

As consumers, voters and policy influencers, we must be conscious *of* and deliberate *about* our demand for Big Mother and Big Butler technology products, particularly with regard to RPA and AI solutions. A healthy human–machine partnership ecosystem demands that we favour these two categories of benevolent intent, and that we protect ourselves from predatory forms of automation at every opportunity.

Driving towards a Big Mother- and Big Butler-inspired future of human–machine partnerships

Innovation, invention and engineering ingenuity have always been most valuable when used in the service of mankind. Even when invention was motivated by profit, as it so often is, the initial benefits to private enterprise and users always spilled over to society at large. Improvements in hunting techniques, animal husbandry, agriculture, craftsmanship, ship-building, civil engineering, refrigeration, medicine, navigation, machine design, production, quality control, computational capabilities, data analytics and automation helped a species of primitive hunter–gatherers master the oceans, conquer scores of infectious diseases, take flight, land robots on alien planets, and imbue inanimate objects with the ability to listen, understand and speak.

One human worker, in partnership with specialized machines, can do the work of hundreds. That is the power and potential of benevolent use cases of human–machine partnerships, and it is worth remembering that humanity is at its best when it focuses on improving its own condition, not when it acts against its own best interests.

It is imperative that we help steer technology developers and implementers towards the pursuit of Big Butler and Big Mother tools.

It is imperative that, as consumers, users of technology, business leaders, decision-makers, policy influencers and technologists, we help steer technology developers and implementers towards the pursuit of Big Butler and Big Mother tools – tools that serve, assist, enhance, augment, expand and improve human capabilities, and open new doors for human potential. We *can* apply the very technologies that threaten to displace millions of workers to help them launch themselves into new pursuits. More importantly, we have a duty to do so.

If we approach the next two decades of innovation, technology implementation and change with the same curiosity, creativity and problem-solving mindset that characterized the Renaissance, the first industrial revolution, the post-war boom and the mobile revolution, we have nothing to fear from the next wave of automation or from the proliferation of artificial intelligence. Quite the contrary. What the next chapter of human civilization tells future generations about us is entirely our choice. With a little luck and a lot of hard work, that chapter will hopefully not be about the mismanagement of innovation, mass unemployment and waves of civil unrest, but rather the first chapter in the new age of human–machine partnerships.

Notes

Chapter 1

1 IPUMS USA (2017) US Bureau of Labor Statistics, McKinsey Global Institute Analysis
2 IPUMS USA (2017) US Bureau of Labor Statistics, McKinsey Global Institute Analysis
3 Orwell, G (1945) *Animal Farm: A fairy story*, Secker and Warburg, London, UK
4 Boulle, P (1963) *La Planète des Singes,* René Julliard, Paris, France
5 Clarke, A C (1968) *2001: A Space Odyssey,* Hutchinson, London, UK
6 Lee, S, Heck, D, Lieber, L and Kirby, J (1969, 2008) *Ironman,* Marvel Studios
7 Larson, G A (1982) *Knight Rider,* NBC
8 United States Department of Labor (2019) Bureau of Labor Statistics, BLS.gov
9 Muro, M, Maxim, R and Whiton, J (2019) *Automation and Artificial Intelligence: How machines are affecting people and places*, Brookings
10 Hawksworth, J, Berriman, R and Saloni, G (2018) *Will Robots Really Steal Our Jobs? An international analysis of the potential long term impact of automation,* PricewaterhouseCoopers
11 Nedelkoska, L and Quintini, G (2018) *Automation, Skills and Training,* OECD

Chapter 2

1 Liszewski, A (2016) Your lonely grandparents can now get a robot retriever to keep them company, 3 October, *Gizmodo*
2 Liszewski, A (2019) We need to talk about this robo-dog companion that Jim Henson's Creature Shop helped design, 18 March, *Gizmodo*

Chapter 3

1 Newman, D and Blanchard, O (2018) *2018 Digital Transformation Index,* Futurum

Chapter 4

1 Newman, D and Blanchard, O (2016) *Building Dragons: Digital transformation in the experience economy*, Broadsuite

2 Newman, D and Blanchard, O (2017) *Futureproof: 7 key pillars for digital transformation success,* Broadsuite

3 Jerde, S (2018) The Walt Disney Company will now use Google technology for its digital ads, 27 November, *Adweek*

4 Newman, D and Blanchard, O (2018) *Digital Transformation Index 2018*, Futurum Research

5 Newman, D and Blanchard, O (2018) *Digital Transformation Index 2018*, Futurum Research

6 Newman, D and Blanchard, O (2019) *5G Readiness and Transformation Index 2019*, Futurum Research

7 Fuze (2017) *Breaking Barriers 2020: How CIOs are shaping the future of work*

8 Newman, D and Blanchard, O (2016) *The Future of Work: Principles of workplace gamification,* Futurum Research

9 Gallup (2017) *State of the Global Workplace*

10 Paynter, B (2019) Poor scheduling costs hourly workers sleep and happiness, 15 February, *Fast Company*

11 Vincent, J (2018) Deep Mind's AI can detect over 50 eye diseases as accurately as a doctor, 13 August, *The Verge*

12 Zarley, B D (2019) Meet the scientists who are training AI to diagnose mental illness, 28 January, *The Verge*

13 Mulvaney, K (2018) *AI can help US unlock the world's most complex operating system: The human body,* 15 October, World Economic Forum

14 Program Ace (2018) Virtual reality in healthcare: A new solution for rehabilitation? 28 February [blog]

15 Moses, L (2017) The *Washington Post*'s robot reporter has published 850 articles in the past year, 14 September, *Digiday*

16 Hornyak, T (2018) The world's first humanless warehouse is run only by robots and is a model for the future, 30 October, CNBC

17 Lawrence, E and Lareau, J (2019) Robot car factory to bring as many as 400 jobs to southeast Michigan, 22 January, Detroit Free Press

18 World Economic Forum (2018) *Future of Jobs Report 2018*

Chapter 5

1 More, T (1516) *Libellus vere aureus, nec minus salutaris quam festivus, de optimo rei publicae statu deque nova insula Utopia*, Habsburg, Netherlands
2 Rose, D (2014) *Enchanted Objects: Design, human desire, and the internet of things*, Scribner, New York

Chapter 6

1 *The Condition of Education: Children and youth with disabilities* (2018) National Center for Educational Statistics, April
2 Humphreys, D and Kelly, P (2014) *How Liberal Arts and Sciences Majors Fare in Employment: A report on earnings and long-term career paths*, American Association of Colleges and Universities (AAC&U) and the National Center for Higher Education Management Systems (NCHEMS)

Chapter 7

1 Morris, D (2017) New French law bars work email after hours, 1 January, *Fortune*
2 Shearer, E and Gottfried, J (2017) *News use across social media platforms 2017*, Pew Research
3 Internet Live Stats (2019) 18 February, www.internetlivestats.com/google-search-statistics/
4 Roberts, J J (2017) Google's $2.7 Billion Fine: What it means and what happens next, 27 June, *Fortune*
5 Kenwright, S (2016) Location World 2016, 11 November [blog]
6 Rawes, E (2018) What is Google Duplex? The smartest chatbot ever, explained, 11 October, *Digital Trends*
7 *Global Status Report on Road Safety* (2018) World Health Organization
8 Dassault Systèmes' living heart project reaches next milestones in mission to improve patient care (2017) 18 October, *Market Insider*

Chapter 8

1 Newman, D and Blanchard, O (2018) *Digital Transformation Index 2018*, Futurum Research
2 Quach, K (2018) Don't try and beat AI, merge with it says chess champ Garry Kasparov, 10 May, *The Register*
3 Markoff, J (2011) Computer wins of 'Jeopardy!': Trivial, it's not, 16 February, *The New York Times*
4 Metz, C (2015) Google's AI wins fifth and final game against Go genius Lee Sedol, 15 March, *Wired*
5 Kleeman, A (2016) Cooking with chef Watson, IBM's artificial-intelligence app, 28 November, *The New Yorker*
6 Hammett, E (2018) How Lexus programmed a machine to write the world's first AI-scripted ad, 16 November, *Marketing Week*
7 Dastin, J (2019) Amazon scraps secret AI recruiting tool that showed bias against women, 9 October, Reuters
8 Amodei, D, Olah, C, Steinhardt, J, Christiano, P, Schulman, J and Mané, D (2017) *Concrete Problems in AI Safety*, Cornell University

Chapter 9

1 Hawksworth, J, Berriman, R and Saloni, G (2018) *Will robots really steal our jobs? An international analysis of the potential long-term impact automation*, PricewaterhouseCoopers
2 Hawksworth, J, Berriman, R and Saloni, G (2018) *Will robots really steal our jobs? An international analysis of the potential long-term impact automation*, PricewaterhouseCoopers
3 Acemonglu, D and Restrepo, P (2018) *Robots and Jobs: Evidence from US labor markets*, 16 July
4 United States Department of Labor: Bureau of Labor Statistics (1996) *Economic News Release: 1995 survey of employer provided training-employer Results*, 10 July
5 United States Department of Labor: Bureau of Labor Statistics (1996) *Economic News Release: 1995 survey of employer provided training-employer results*, 10 July
6 Wandner, S (2012) *The Response of the US Public Workforce System to High Unemployment during the Great Recession*, September, Urban Institute

Index

5G 106–07

accelerated micro-innovation 59, 60
accounting/accountants 80–81, 215
adaptation 14–15, 211
    businesses 67–68
    to disruption 42–44
    educational institutions 146–48
    workers 100–02, 108–09
administrators 217
adoption of disruptive
        technology 43–44
agency, individual 177–79, 180
agility 71–73, 108, 192
agriculture 7, 81, 217
algorithmic wave 18–19
algorithms 88–89
    search engines and recommendation
        engines 154–56
Amazon 125, 186–87, 203, 231
analogue tools and skills 132–34
analytics tools 113–15
animal–human partnerships 8–9
archetypal technologies 35–38
    technology companies and product
        design 196–200
    see also under individual names
architects 214
artificial intelligence (AI) 1–2, 53,
        55–56, 63
    AI bias 110–11, 115–17, 203–05
    digital assistants 157–60, 230–31
    healthcare 173–74
    limitations 201–03
    remote learning, mixed reality and
        educational institutions 135–38
    real-world 9–10
arts subjects 129–30, 134, 142–43,
        148–49
Associated Press 89
augmentation 48, 49, 210–11, 220–21

correct balance with automation for
        businesses 73–76
    human augmentation robotics for
        blue-collar workers 120–21
    of oneself 103–04
    technology companies and designing
        for 200–06
    workers 102–04
augmentation wave 18–19
augmented reality (AR)
    blue-collar jobs 119–20
    in shopping 170–71
autonomous vehicles 10–14,
        163–66, 205
autonomous wave 18–19
awareness 100–02, 107, 118, 124

balance
    between analogue and digital
        tools 132–34
    between augmentation and
        automation 73–76
benevolent technologies 231–33
    predatory technologies and 228–31
    see also Big Butler technologies; Big
        Mother technologies
Berriman, Richard 18–20
bias, AI 110–11, 115–17, 203–05
Big Brother technologies 35–36, 37,
        62, 189–90, 196–200, 228–31
Big Butler technologies 35–38, 62, 155,
        183–84, 189–90, 196–200
    future of human–machine
        partnerships 228–33
Big Mother technologies 35–36, 37,
        62, 184, 189–90, 196–200
    future of human–machine
        partnerships 228–33
black-hat technology companies 198,
        199–200
blockchain technologies 52

blue-collar jobs/workers 104–05, 117–22
  options for 118–22
  transitioning to smart-automation operator jobs 117–18
broad portfolio of technologies 111–13
businesses 65–95, 139–40, 192
  AI bias and business functions 204–05
  applying change management principles 71–73
  balance between automation and augmentation 73–76
  benefits of synergy between humans and machines 94–95
  digital transformation roadmap 65–68
  enterprise-class 54–56, 94, 95
  framing expectations 54–57
  hiring and training 92–93
  involvement in education and training 144–46
  IT and HR 76–79
  management 82–83
  SMBs/SMEs 56–57, 94–95
  steps to transforming 69–71
  types of human–machine partnerships to prioritize 79–92
BYOA (bring your own app) 76
BYOD (bring your own device) 76

car ownership 165–66
  see also autonomous vehicles
career futureproofing 97–100
categories of automation see archetypal technologies
cause-and-effect modelling 31–35
centralized IT 76
change management principles 71–73
checkouts 168–69
city management 83–84
city planning 83–84
civil engineers 214
Class VR 136
collar colours 104–05, 119
combat drones 205
commercial drivers 10–14, 219–20
company evolution 70–71

consequences 32–35
consolidation of jobs/roles 15–21
construction 84–85
consumers 50–51, 153–84
  digital assistants 157–60, 230–31
  framing expectations 61–62
  healthcare and homecare 171–75
  home automation 160–63, 170
  impact of human–machine partnerships in daily lives 153–54
  life planning 179–80
  lifestyles and relationships 176–79
  personal safety and privacy 52, 62, 180–83, 230–31
  recommendation engines 154–56, 171
  shopping 167–71
  transportation and infrastructure 163–66
  trust 156–57, 177
continuous training 149–52
cost-benefit analysis 30–32
  inclusion of consequences 32–35
cost centre, IT as 77–78
culture 144–46
customer service professionals 219
customized curricula 137

Dassault Systèmes 174
data security and privacy 52, 62, 180–83, 230–31
data validators 115–17
decentralized IT 76–77
decision-makers 113–15, 212
decision-making 205–06, 220
design intent 193–96
digital assistants 157–60, 230–31
digital transformation 54–56
  roadmap 65–68
Disney 66–67, 145
displacement 207–09, 211
  retraining following 224–28
disruption 38–40, 47–48
  adaptation to 42–44
diverse portfolio of technologies 111–13
drivers, professional 10–14, 219–20

Duplex 159–60
dwellings 4–5
    home automation 160–63, 170

edge computing 106–07
educational institutions 53, 127–52
    adaptation 146–48
    business involvement 144–46
    case for rebooting education
        129–30
    continuous training 149–52
    difference between education and
        training 128–29
    economic considerations 139–41
    elementary education 132–34
    framing expectations 60–61
    function defined by form and
        purpose 131–32
    liberal arts 142–43, 148–49
    need for radical change 127–28
    remote learning, mixed reality and
        AI 135–38
    secondary education 134–35
    subjects see subjects, educational
    transition to mass
        automation 214–15
    universities 141–44, 145–46
efficiency 41, 74
eldercare 88
elementary education 132–34
employment
    changing nature of 58
    see also jobs; work
end of work 53
engineers 213–14
enhancement 4–5, 14–16, 39–42, 43,
    210–11, 220–21
enterprise-class organizations 54–56,
    94, 95
entertainment 85–86
entrepreneurialism 59, 95
evaluation of human–machine
        partnerships 29–45
    adaptation 42–44
    archetypal categories 35–38
    cost-benefit analysis 30–32
    disruption 38–40, 47–48
    involving consequences 32–35

evolution
    company evolution 70–71
    evolutionary response to smart
        automation 25–27
exoskeletons 84, 120–21
expectations, framing see framing
        expectations

Facebook 231
facial recognition technologies 186–87,
    188, 229–30
farmers/farming 81, 217
financial planning 80–81
framing expectations 47–63
    beyond the next 10 years 52–54
    businesses 54–57
    consumers 61–62
    education and training 60–61
    predictions for human–machine
        partnerships 48–52
    technology companies 62–63
    workers 57–60
Frankenstein (Shelley) 187–88
free-associating collaboration 59
'friend vs foe' analysis 35
full body power suits 84, 121
funding education 139–41
future of human–machine
        partnerships 207–33
    benevolent and predatory
        technologies 228–31
    driving towards benevolent
        technologies 231–33
    ideal 209–21
    societal and legal
        framework 221–28
futureproofing careers 97–100

gamification 79
genius 41–42
geofenced ecosystems 91
gig economy 143
Google 155, 186–87, 231
    Duplex 159–60
governments 186–88
green-collar jobs 119
grey-collar jobs 104, 105
grey probabilities 114–15

harm minimization 185–86
Hasbro 33
Hawksworth, John 18–20
healthcare 86–88, 171–75, 216–17
Heliograf 89
high-value tasks/roles 22–25, 210
hiring 92–93
history of human–machine
    partnerships 1–27
    automation and increasing human
        potential 21–23
    evolutionary response to smart
        automation 25–27
    impact of automation on
        employment 1–2, 6–9
    impact of smart automation on
        professional drivers 10–14
    job consolidation due to smart
        automation 15–21
    new tools and enhancements 14–16
    real-world AI 9–10
    shift from low-value tasks to high-
        value tasks 23–25
    smart automation 5–7
    task automation vs job
        automation 12–14
    tools and enhancements 1–5
home automation 160–63, 170
homecare 88, 171–75
    technicians 216–17
hospice care technicians 216–17
human augmentation *see* augmentation
human augmentation robotics 120–21
human resources (HR) 88–89
    IT and 76–79
    managers 219
human skills and traits 21–23, 41–42,
    109–11, 126, 129–30
human-to-machine ratios 223

ideal future 209–21
individual agency 177–79, 180
inflection point 51
information, accessing and
    consuming 154–56
information workers 115–17
infrastructure, transportation 11,
    163–66
initiative 100–02, 107, 109, 118, 124

innovation 41–42
institutional framework 221–28
Intel 157
intent, design 193–96
interfaces 50, 51, 107, 157–58
Internet of Things (IoT) 51, 63, 106–07
IT (information technology)
    and HR 76–79
    need to be embedded in
        businesses 65–68
    professionals 217–18

job training *see* training
Job Training Partnership Act (JTPA)
    226, 227
jobs
    at risk of automation 16–21, 48–49
    consolidation of 15–21
    declining 93
    displacement *see* displacement
    impact of automation 1–2, 6–9,
        207–09
    new and emerging 49–50, 93
    not easily automated 118–19
    replacement 39–42, 48–49, 190–93,
        211, 220–21
    task automation vs job
        automation 12–14
    technology companies and job
        losses due to automation
        190–93
    waves of automation 18–19
journalism 89–90
Judah, Norm 110–11
judgement 110, 113–14

keys 160–61

law enforcement agencies 186–88, 215
lawmakers 188–89, 222
lawyers 215
leadership 41–42, 126
    political leaders 188–89
    team leaders 212–13
legal framework 221–28
legitimacy of educational
    institutions 150
leveraging smart automation
    105–08, 124

liberal arts education 142–43, 148–49
life planning 179–80
lifestyles 176–79
light switches 160–61
logistics 91–92
loneliness 162–63
low-value tasks 22, 23, 25, 210
lowest wage jobs 17

machine operators and assemblers 19, 20–21
maintenance 122
   technicians 214
management and managers 210–11, 221
   businesses 82–83
   cities 83–84
   human resources managers 219
   middle executives/managers 113–15, 212–13
   plant managers 214
   senior executives/managers 113–15, 212
manual work 23–24, 117–22
manufacturing 7, 91–92
   plant automation 208–09
maths 129, 134
Maxim, Robert 16–18
McDonald's 145
medical research 87, 174–75
methods 144–46
middle executives/managers 113–15, 212–13
military forces 186–88
mixed reality
   education 135–38
   workers 119–20
More, Sir Thomas 99
Muro, Mark 16–18

Nedelkoska, Ljubica 23–24
new and emerging jobs 49–50, 93
news reporting 89–90
next-collar jobs 108–13
not-easily-automated jobs 118–19
nurses 216–17

omnichannel experiences 169
on-demand continuous
   training 149–52

operating systems, standardization
   of 91
operational efficiency 41, 74
opposable thumb 3
order-fulfilment centres 169–70

patient management AIs 173
personal safety and privacy 52, 62, 180–83, 230–31
personalized curricula 137
pets, robotic 33
physical well-being,
   monitoring 161–63
physicians 216
pink-collar jobs 104
planning
   cities 83–84
   financial 80–81
   life planning 179–80
plant and maintenance
   technicians 214
plant managers 214
political leaders 188–89
power suits 84, 121
predatory technologies 228–31
   see also Big Brother technologies
predictive analytics 113–15
prescriptive management tools
   113–15
presence 135–38
privacy 52, 62, 180–83, 230–31
private–public partnerships 144–46
proactiveness 43–44, 72–73
problem-solving 2–4, 14, 35, 38
   education and 132–33
   technology companies and 194–96
product design 149
   technology companies and 193–206
professional drivers 10–14, 219–20
professionals 19, 20–21
   education and training 143–44, 145–47
programming, teaching 133
purpose
   of education 131–32
   of evaluation 30
   questions for technology
     companies 193–96

Quintini, Glenda 23–24

random attacks on robots 13
recommendation engines 154–56, 171
relationships 176–79
remote learning 135–38
repair 122
replacement 39–42, 48–49, 211, 220–21
    technology companies and 190–93
resources 100–02, 107, 124–25
responsibility 186–88
retail 92
    transformation of shopping 167–71
    transition to mass automation 218
    workers 122–23
retraining 224–28
return on investment (ROI) 44
robotic pets 33
robotic process automation (RPA) 82–83, 92
role transitions 22–25, 210, 212–20
Rose, David 106

safety 52, 62, 180–83, 230–31
Saloni, Goel 18–20
scans, medical 87
science 129, 134
search engines 154–56
secondary education 134–35
security 51, 62, 180–83, 230–31
selective automation 74–75
self-augmentation 103–04
senior executives/managers 113–15, 212
sensor technology 172
Shelley, Mary 187–88
shopping 167–71
shopping lists 170
small to medium-sized businesses/ enterprises (SMBs/SMEs) 56–57, 94–95
smart appliances 170
smart automation 1–2, 5–7
    evolutionary response 25–27
    impact on professional drivers 10–14
    and job consolidation 15–21
    leveraging by workers 105–08, 124
smart home automation 160–63, 170

smart objects 51
    elementary education and 132–34
societal framework 221–28
soft skills 21–23, 41–42, 109–11, 126, 129–30
software-as-a-service (SaaS) offerings 94
space, arrangement of 131, 135
special needs, students with 137
specialized employees 213
specialized smart-automation operator jobs 117–18
specialized white-collar occupations 215
standardization of operating systems 91
STEM jobs 58
subjects, educational 129–30, 134
    essential new subjects 138–39
    liberal arts 142–43, 148–49
surgeons 216
surgery 86–87
surgical robots 86–87, 173, 174, 175
surveillance technologies 186–87, 198, 229–31
systems management 122

tasks
    automation 12–14, 15, 75–76, 195–96
    low-value and high-value tasks/ roles 22–25, 210
taxation 224
team leaders 212–13
technological adaptation see adaptation
technological agility 71–73, 108, 192
technological archetypes see archetypal technologies
technological literacy 50
    leaders and lawmakers 182, 188–89
technology categories 68
    identifying 69
technology companies 185–206
    avoiding becoming a Big Brother company 189–90
    design intent 193–96
    designing for augmentation 200–06

designing for Big Brother, Big
    Butler and Big Mother
    technologies 196–200
duty to minimize harm 185–86
framing expectations 62–63
involvement in education and
    training 145–46, 147
job loss problem related to
    automation 190–93
and leaders and lawmakers 188–89
questions to be asked 193–96
responsibility 186–88
technology partners 69–70
telemedicine 172
time 22, 168, 176, 210–11
tools 3–4, 14–16, 63
traffic-related accidents 166
training 53, 60–61
    accessing by workers 124–25
    difference from education 128–29
    for a new class of machine-adjacent
        roles 92–93
    on-demand continuous 149–52
    retraining for displaced
        workers 224–28
    technology companies and 191–93
    universities shifting focus to 41–44
    see also educational institutions
transformation of work 53–54
transition to mass automation 212–20
transportation 10–14, 163–66, 205
trust 156–57, 177, 206

uncertainty 48
    grey probabilities 114–15
unintended consequences 32–35
universal basic income (UBI) 53,
    98–99, 223
universities 141–44, 145–46
USA Today 89
user, design for the 193–94

V2I system 163–64
V2P system 163–64

V2V system 163–64
value of human–machine
    partnerships 44–45
values 144–46
virtual reality (VR)
    blue-collar jobs 119–20
    in shopping 170–71
vision 41–42
visual effects (VFX) 85–86
voice interfaces 50, 51, 107,
    157–58

warehouses/warehousing 91–92,
    208–09
Washington Post 89
waves of job automation 18–19
weaponization of technologies 177,
    187, 229–31
weapons manufacturers 197
white-collar jobs 104–05, 215
white-hat technology
    companies 199–200
Whiton, Jacob 16–18
work
    end of 53
    transformation of
        53–54, 58–59
    see also jobs
workers 53, 97–126, 191
    adaptation 100–02,
        108–09
    augmentation 102–04
    collar colours 104–05, 119
    framing expectations 57–60
    futureproofing careers
        97–100
    key job categories 113–23
    leveraging smart
        automation 105–08, 124
    preparing for the AI-driven
        economy 108–13
    self-augmentation 103–04
World Economic Forum
    (WEF) 92–93